# Effective Educational Environments

# Effective Educational Environments

Jean Stockard
Maralee Mayberry

CORWIN PRESS, INC.
A Sage Publications Company
Newbury Park, California

*For information address:*

Corwin Press, Inc.
A Sage Publications Company
2455 Teller Road
Newbury Park, California 91320

SAGE Publications Ltd.
6 Bonhill Street
London EC2A 4PU
United Kingdom

SAGE Publications India Pvt. Ltd.
M-32 Market
Greater Kailash I
New Delhi 110048 India

Printed in the United States of America

**Library of Congress Cataloging-in-Publication Data**

Stockard, Jean
Effective educational environments / Jean Stockard, Maralee Mayberry.
p. cm.
Includes bibliographical references (p. ) and index.
ISBN 0-8039-6011-5. — ISBN 0-8039-6012-3 (pbk.)
1. School environment—United States. 2. Classroom environment—United States. 3. Academic achievement—United States. 4. Community and school—United States. 5. Educational sociology—United States. I. Mayberry, Maralee. II. Title.
LC210.5.S76 1992
370.19—dc20 92-417
CIP

92 93 94 95 96 10 9 8 7 6 5 4 3 2 1

Corwin Press Production Editor: Tara S. Mead

# Contents

# Preface

Each year, politicians and social activists expound on the problems of our schools. Parents worry about the educational experiences of their children. Social scientists from a wide range of disciplines study the nature of schools and students' experiences in schools. Over the last four decades, a wide variety of educational critiques have been published. In the early 1950s, they focused on the problems with "progressive education," while in the late 1950s, the launching of Sputnik prompted a number of curriculum reforms. The 1960s saw the reaction to James Coleman and associates' (1966) quantitative *Equality of Educational Opportunity* report and the more qualitative writings of critics such as John Holt (1964, 1967), Jonathon Kozol (1967), and James Herndon (1968, 1971). The 1970s saw the development of various alternative schools, and the early 1980s witnessed large-scale critiques of high schools by people such as Ernest Boyer (1983), Theodore Sizer (1984), and John Goodlad (1984). (See Gregory and Smith 1987, pp. 6-23, for an extensive discussion of these critiques.) Most recently, reformers have called for standardized, nationwide testing of students and greater regulation of the curriculum (Finn 1991). Clearly, both the general public and the scholars specializing in the study of education are concerned with students' academic achievement.

Notably enough, virtually all of these critiques have looked at pedagogical techniques and the content of the curriculum rather than the environments in which students learn (see

Gregory and Smith 1987). Yet these learning environments have an important impact on students' achievement. The composition and size of the groups in which students learn; the facilities in which they learn; their climate or culture, that is, the predominant norms and values; and their community environment all affect students' learning. These effects occur over and above students' individual characteristics such as their family background. In this book, we review the empirical literature describing these environmental influences, noting both its problems and its promises. We then show how long-standing theoretical traditions in the social sciences can be used to integrate the material into a simple, yet inclusive conceptual framework that is useful for both policymakers and researchers.

## Why Study Learning Environments?

Much of the early research on student achievement focused on variables related to individual students. A large number of studies have documented the important effect of students' ability, attitudes, and beliefs on their achievement, finding that students' feelings of self-efficacy, or locus of control, are extremely important in accounting for higher achievement (see Coleman et al. 1966). The literature has also documented the influence of parents' economic well-being, educational background, and concern and involvement with their children's education (see Shea 1976; Bridge et al. 1979; Mosteller and Moynihan 1972, for reviews of this literature). These studies consistently indicate that students with greater measured ability, with more positive attitudes toward education, and with higher-status and more concerned parents have higher achievement.

Although these variables have a large influence on the achievement of individual students, they are primarily related to institutions such as the economy and the family rather than education. Individuals' educational resources and economic forces, such as the supply of jobs and possible discrimination within the labor market, tend to determine the socioeconomic resources of individual families. Family interaction patterns, norms, and values are important influences on measured ability and students' attitudes and beliefs. These variables are largely beyond the control of school officials and policymakers.

Although a number of authors have tried to discount the influence that schools have on achievement (Averch et al. 1974 is seen as one of the first and most influential of these statements), a great deal of evidence suggests that schools, as well as families, influence students' achievement as well as their attitudes toward learning. The easiest way to see the effect of schooling is simply to compare learning that occurs when students have schooling with what occurs when they do not. A number of studies indicate that students who have completed more levels of schooling clearly have greater cognitive development than those who have not (e.g., Alexander et al. 1985; Shavit and Featherman 1988; see also Meyer 1980; Husen and Tuijnman 1991). Similarly, students show more cognitive growth while they are in school than while they are on vacation (Heyns 1978). More important, however, schools can vary in quality; and students in higher-quality schools have higher achievement than those in poorer-quality schools, even when they have similar family and individual characteristics. Most of our review in later chapters focuses on these differences between schools and what we term *educational* or *learning environments*.

## Why Focus on Student Achievement?

A number of studies, primarily those in the status attainment tradition, have noted that eventual adult success, in terms of occupational attainment and income, actually depends more on educational attainment than on educational achievement. In other words, adult success depends more on the number of years one goes to school than on how much one learns in school. Completion of certain levels of schooling, more than simply learning a given amount of material, facilitates entry into occupations (e.g., Hauser 1971; Blau and Duncan 1967; Sewell and Shah 1968; Jencks et al. 1979). This reflects the effect of certification and the relationship that modern societies have developed between successful completion of a given training experience and job entrance, often wholly apart from the actual requirements of the job itself (see Collins 1979).

One could then well ask why we have chosen to focus on student achievement, rather than simply educational attainment, in this book. One obvious reason is that most of the literature on learning environments has used student achievement as the dependent variable. We do report results that use other measures, such as educational aspirations and attainment as dependent variables, but these studies are relatively less common than those that focus on achievement.

Beyond such matters of convenience, we also believe that it is proper to focus on student achievement because this embodies the given goal of schools. The major task of schools is to educate students, to provide them with the fundamental knowledge and skills deemed necessary for survival in the modern world. We are interested in how the environments in which students learn either impede or facilitate this task.

In addition, it is possible that increased academic achievement can result in a better quality of life for students as they enter adulthood. Even though enhanced academic achievement may not be directly linked to the attainment of a more equitable society (see Jencks et al. 1972), it is possible that it may ultimately result in pressures for a more equitable occupational and income structure as those with requisite skills and knowledge are increasingly denied positions for which they are qualified. For instance, a fair amount of cross-cultural evidence suggests that increasing educational attainment of women in a society is a necessary, although not a sufficient, condition for increased demands for equality in other institutional sectors. Women's greater educational equality promotes dissatisfaction with their lesser status in other areas, which in turn prompts calls for greater equality in these sectors (see Stockard and Johnson 1992).

## Overview of the Book

In our review of the literature on environmental influences, we deal with four major areas: groupings of students, learning climates, school facilities and size, and community environments. We have tried to review the highest-quality work that is available, focusing on studies with larger samples and better methodologies and frequently relying on meta-analyses and detailed reviews of extensive literature. We have also tried to look for patterns of results, rather than simply using one or two unusual studies, to ensure that our conclusions are more reliable. Our discussion of the literature is nontechnical and should be accessible to all readers. At the same time, we include extensive references to the original research for those interested in additional details.

Any review of the literature is, of course, only a snapshot of the knowledge available at a given time. Some of the literature that we present comes from areas in which there are intense controversies and sharply worded debates. We have tried to weigh this evidence and present, as much as possible, general conclusions from this work and references to various participants in the debates. Certainly, as research findings continue to accumulate, at least some of the evidence we present here may be challenged and modified. We believe, however, that the conclusions we present represent the general state of knowledge regarding learning environments at the current time.

In Chapter 1, we examine the vast literature regarding how the composition of educational groups affects learning. Literature in this area has examined the racial, socioeconomic, and ability context in which students learn, often focusing on the racial and ethnic desegregation of schools and classrooms, socioeconomic segregation of schools, and ability tracking and grouping. More recent literature has also looked at the effect of the gender composition of schools. In general, this literature suggests that the composition of students within a learning situation can influence students' achievement, and, with the exception of gender composition, more heterogeneous environments enhance learning.

Much of the literature on compositional effects avoids studying *how* the group's composition affects student learning. We suggest that this influence involves, at least partially, the nature of the "learning climate" of the classroom and school. Chapter 2 focuses on these learning climates and cultures—the norms and values that characterize learning environments. We describe various ways researchers have approached this area and then summarize current views regarding the effect of school and classroom climates on student learning. The literature consistently indicates that schools and classrooms that have strong academic norms, an orderly environment, supportive and effective leadership, and warm, supportive interpersonal relationships have higher achievement.

Although Chapters 1 and 2 deal more with social and psychological variables, Chapter 3 moves to a somewhat different level: the physical environment of schools. In this chapter, we examine how school facilities and expenditures, teachers' qualifications, and school and classroom size affect students' achievement. Although a number of reviews have noted that these variables have no effect on student achievement, we show that research that employs adequate methodology indicates that both smaller schools and smaller classrooms enhance student achievement. In addition, the resources that students have, especially the amount of time allocated for instruction and learning and their teachers' instructional skills, affect achievement.

The community environment of schools may at first appear as intractable as family background variables. Yet, in fact, practices of school consolidation, school closures, and the construction of new schools, as well as policies regarding parental and community involvement, are all controlled by policymakers. These policies directly influence the relationship between schools and their communities. Thus, in Chapter 4, we examine the way in which the community environment influences students' achievement. We show how closer ties between schools and parents and other community members can enhance achievement.

There have been several attempts to synthesize literature regarding the influence of at least some environmental variables on student achievement. Although there is a long theoretical tradition, in both psychology and sociology, regarding the influence of the social context or environment on individual behavior, reviews of the educational literature, however, have generally not taken this theoretical tradition into account. Instead, they have tended simply to describe empirical results and/or present large-scale models of interacting influences on achievement (e.g., Centra and Potter 1980). Although we believe that such descriptions can be extremely useful, we also believe that a more parsimonious and a more analytical description of environmental influences on student achievement can be obtained by using the theoretical traditions developed within the social sciences. These theories are general descriptions of social behavior that have been developed to explain and predict behavior in a wide variety of settings. They are thus much more flexible and, we believe, valid than relatively ad hoc theoretical explanations often developed to explain student learning.

In Chapter 5, we briefly describe theoretical traditions from sociology and psychology that deal with environmental influences on many kinds of behaviors and show how these views can be used to analyze influences on learning. We then summarize this literature in a simple conceptual framework that emphasizes both how members of a school create the prevailing social order or climate through their relationships and social actions and how, in turn, this social order influences individuals' actions. We suggest that this model can account for the many research findings reviewed in Chapters 1 through 4, yet it is parsimonious and useful for practitioners and policymakers.

In Chapter 6, we explore the implications of our review for policy and social change. We believe that policymakers, administrators, teachers, students, parents, and community members can create more effective schools and classrooms at relatively low cost. These changes would not only enhance achievement but produce more humane learning environments for all school participants.

## Audience for the Book

We hope that this book will be read and used by educational policymakers, educational administrators, principals, and teachers as well as parents and academics who are interested in what the research community can contribute to their thinking and decision making about policy-related issues. We believe that it can also be a useful supplement in seminars and courses in educational policy, educational administration, and sociology of education that deal with the development of effective educational environments.

## Acknowledgments

Our work on this project began with an institutional grant from the National Institute of Education-sponsored Center for Educational Policy and Management at the University of Oregon several years ago and we are very grateful for that support. Since that time, a number of people have provided encouragement and assistance of various kinds. We especially want to thank Robert Mattson, Paul Goldman, Richard Hersh, Joe Stone, Marian Jacobs, Leonard Gordon, Sally Bowman, Robert O'Brien, Samuel Bacharach, Maureen Hallinan, Mary Freer, Ann Hrabacka, Barbara Luton, and members of the sociology department at the University of Nevada. Jean Stockard also wishes to thank the members of her family—Walt, Beth, John, and Tim Wood—for their personal support. Maralee Mayberry wishes to thank Joseph Finkhouse, who has been a constant source of encouragement and ideas. Any errors that may remain in the manuscript are, of course, our own responsibility.

JEAN STOCKARD
*University of Oregon*

MARALEE MAYBERRY
*University of Nevada—Las Vegas*

# About the Authors

**Jean Stockard** is Professor of Sociology at the University of Oregon in Eugene, where she also holds an appointment within the Division of Educational Policy and Management. Her major interests lie in the areas of sociology of education, sociology of gender, and methodology. Her most recent book is *Sex and Gender in Society* (Prentice-Hall, 1992), written with Miriam Johnson. Some of her articles have appeared in the *American Educational Research Journal, Educational Administration Quarterly, Social Psychology Quarterly, Sex Roles,* and *Journal of Vocational Behavior.* Her current research focuses on the development of occupational choice among boys and girls.

**Maralee Mayberry** is Assistant Professor of Sociology at the University of Nevada, Las Vegas. Her major interests lie in the areas of sociology of education and political sociology. Her current research focuses on the home school movement and the development of cooperative relations between families and schools. She and her colleagues are conducting an ongoing study of home schools in four western states funded by the U.S. Department of Education. One aspect of the study examines effective learning climates in the home school and the effects of community and parent involvement on educational achievement. Her articles have appeared in *Education and Urban Society, Educational Review, The Urban Review,* and *The Home School Researcher.*

# 1

# Groupings of Students

By definition, schools instruct students in groups. Because there are always far more pupils than teachers, educators have devised a number of ways of grouping students for more efficient instruction. Within a given district, students attend different schools, based on their grade level and, often, the location of their residence. Within schools, students are grouped not just by grade levels but often by curricular track and by ability.

Federal laws and court decisions within the last three and a half decades have compelled many districts to develop school attendance policies that enhance the racial integration of schools, thus promoting greater diversity in race and ethnicity and, although usually as only a by-product of racial integration, in social class. In contrast, within-school grouping, where students are placed in tracks and ability groups with others judged to have similar abilities, is designed to promote greater homogeneity. It is generally believed that these more homogeneous within-school groupings enhance achievement by allowing teachers to alter the curriculum and instructional approach to best reach different types of students as well as by protecting less capable students from extensive contact with brighter peers that might lower their self-concepts and create negative attitudes toward learning (see Oakes 1985, 1987; Hallinan 1987, pp. 41-42; Barr and Dreeben 1983).

In this chapter, we review literature that examines the influence of student grouping on educational outcomes, focusing first on variations between schools and then on within-school and within-classroom groupings. Although it must be remembered that much research still remains to be done in this area, our analysis of the currently available literature generally suggests that more heterogeneous instructional groups produce the greatest achievement gains, especially for those not in the highest groups. Explanations of these results focus both on variations in instructional practices and on group norms and expectations regarding behaviors. The composition of an instructional setting, whether a school, a classroom, or a smaller learning group, seems to be highly related to students' and teachers' assumptions about the capabilities of group members, to students' behaviors and aspirations, and to teachers' instructional practices.

## Between-School Differences and Educational Outcomes

The composition of the student body may vary a great deal from school to school. Some schools primarily serve higher-status, white students, and some primarily serve lower-status students of racial and ethnic minorities. Some schools have many students with high ability; others have students with a broader range of abilities or a majority with more limited skills. Virtually all public schools in the United States are now coeducational, but a few, especially parochial schools, enroll only boys or girls. In this section, we review literature that documents the relationship of the composition of a school's student body to educational outcomes. We focus first on the influence of the racial-ethnic composition of a school on minority students' achievement and then move to a discussion of other compositional variables, including the socioeconomic status of the students, their average ability, and their sex.

## DESEGREGATION AND ACHIEVEMENT

Efforts to desegregate schools in the United States are now more than a quarter century old. Although the situation varies from one part of the country to another, national data indicate that schools in the 1990s are about as desegregated as they were in 1972. A third of all African American children are in schools with 90% or greater minority enrollment, and the number of Hispanic children in segregated schools has actually increased since the late 1960s (Schofield 1991). A great deal of research has examined the effects of school desegregation on both students' social relationships and their academic achievement (e.g., Armor 1972; Pettigrew and Green 1976). The results are not totally clear cut, often because researchers have used varying definitions of desegregation and have employed varied means of studying the process and outcomes (see Schofield 1991). In general, the results are much stronger when experimental and longitudinal designs are used and when younger children are involved (Crain and Mahard 1983; Mahard and Crain 1983; see also St. John 1975; Bradley and Bradley 1977).

A number of studies have used nationwide survey data from the large-scale *Equality of Educational Opportunity* (EEO) study (Coleman et al. 1966), which included both newly desegregated schools and those that were "naturally" integrated, serving neighborhoods that were either integrated or segregated but adjacent. These studies have found that, for minority students, but not white students, having more white classmates is associated with higher achievement and later educational attainment (see Bridge et al. 1979, pp. 231-32). This is generally explained by the higher status of the white classmates (see the discussion below on socioeconomic context). Later studies, some using survey data but others employing more complex designs, have focused somewhat more on the experiences of students in newly desegregated settings. Although some of these more recent studies show few effects, those that have used randomized experimental designs and that have focused on minority students who entered desegregated settings at lower grade levels have produced even stronger evidence of the benefits of desegregation for at least some groups of students.

From their review of a number of studies judged to be methodologically strong, Mahard and Crain (1983, p. 111) conclude that desegregation enhances minority students' achievement with an estimated effect equal to about a quarter of a standard deviation or 0.3 of a grade year. In addition, desegregation appears to raise African American children's IQ test scores by an average of about 4 points, an increase that "would erase nearly half of the gap between that and the norm of 100" (Mahard and Crain 1983, p. 115).

The achievement increases that come from attending desegregated schools appear to be stronger than those that come from enrollment in compensatory education programs (Weinberg 1983). In addition, attendance at desegregated schools appears to have lifelong benefits. Extensive longitudinal studies now available indicate that minority students who attend desegregated schools are much more likely to attend desegregated colleges, work in desegregated jobs, live in desegregated neighborhoods, and have cross-race friendships (Braddock et al. 1984; Braddock and Dawkins 1984).

The effects of desegregation seem to depend on a number of variables involving the way in which the process occurs. The importance of early desegregation is clear. Many studies find achievement gains only for African American children who attend desegregated schools in the primary years, and the most positive results occur for those who begin desegregated schooling in kindergarten. Starting desegregated schooling in middle school or high school is much less likely to have a positive effect. In addition, a fair amount of evidence suggests that African American students' achievement is enhanced in desegregated schools only when there is a "critical mass" of black students. When minority students make up less than 20% of the student body, the beneficial effects of desegregation are generally not apparent (Mahard and Crain 1983).

Perhaps most important, minority achievement in desegregated schools is enhanced where "the racial attitudes of the staff and the overall racial climate of the classroom are more positive" (Mahard and Crain 1983, p. 105; see also Schofield and Sagar 1983). Several authors suggest that curricular materials that promote multicultural awareness and classroom and extracurricular activities that enhance cross-race cooperation help promote this favorable climate (Schofield 1991, p. 370;

Schofield and Sagar 1983). The within-school and classroom grouping practices of tracking and ability grouping, as well as seemingly voluntary grouping by students into extracurricular activities, can sometimes lead to resegregation of racial and ethnic groups within a school and classroom. These practices may be well intentioned, prompted by the assumption that grouping helps both teachers and students or the belief that students should be allowed to choose their activities. Yet they can actually work against other goals of developing more cooperative and extensive cross-race relationships (see Eyler et al. 1983; also Patchen 1982).

Explanations of the effect of desegregation on achievement tend to focus both on how characteristics of the minority students' classmates in integrated schools affect classroom interactions as well as on social-psychological benefits that arise from the experience of being in an integrated school (Crain 1971). Patchen's extensive study of desegregated schools in one city suggests that academic discipline standards are higher in desegregated classrooms, with all students expected to show higher achievement (Patchen 1982, p. 326). Other authors suggest that the desegregated classroom may be more cognitively stimulating, with students exposed to a variety of experiences and behaviors that they would not find in a more homogeneous setting (Mahard and Crain 1983, pp. 115-17).

In addition, however, simply being in a desegregated setting conveys certain messages to minority children. The extensive 1966 EEO report (Coleman et al. 1966) found that the most important influences on students' achievement were their interest in learning, academic self-concept, and locus of control—a perception that they could control their lives. Nancy St. John (1975) has suggested that segregated schooling gives a "symbolic message," conveying to children what it is possible for them to expect from life. Conceivably, minority children in desegregated schools are much more likely than their peers in segregated schools to perceive that they have greater control over their lives and that there are more possibilities for them. In this way, experiences in desegregated schools help prompt achievement by enhancing students' locus of control, thus prompting them to behave in purposive, achievement-related manners (Mahard and Crain 1983, pp. 110-24).

## SCHOOL COMPOSITION AND ACHIEVEMENT

A number of researchers have documented a relationship between the composition of a school's student body and individual students' educational achievement and aspirations, often called a "contextual" effect. This research has focused on the socioeconomic composition of schools, their ability composition, and their sex composition.

*Socioeconomic context.* In the United States, the racial composition of a school is usually highly associated with its socioeconomic composition. Schools that are largely white are also likely to include more students of middle-class background, and schools with more minority students are more likely to include students of working- and lower-class backgrounds. Many studies have focused specifically on the effect of a school's socioeconomic context by examining the relationship between the average characteristics of students in a classroom or school and student achievement and aspirations. The results generally suggest that students from schools with more higher-status classmates have higher achievement, better school attendance, and higher aspirations. These findings appear even when students' individual ability levels and socioeconomic status are controlled. In other words, students from lower-status families or with lower ability levels tend to have better educational outcomes when they attend schools that include more students from a higher socioeconomic background than when they attend schools that are predominantly attended by those from lower-status backgrounds (Alexander and Eckland 1975; Alexander et al. 1979; Alwin and Otto 1977; Bain and Anderson 1974; Blau 1960; Bowles and Gintis 1976; Boyle 1966; Coleman et al. 1966; Michael 1961; Mortimore et al. 1988; Nelson 1972; Sewell and Armer 1966; Turner 1964; Wilson 1959).

A number of authors have tried to explain how the socioeconomic context affects educational outcomes. (See Alwin and Otto 1977; Alexander et al. 1979; Sewell and Armer 1966; Hauser 1971; Dreeben and Gamoran 1986, for examples.) One set of explanations focuses on the characteristics of a student's peers and how these vary across schools with different socioeconomic contexts. In schools with a higher socioeconomic context, students simply have a greater probability of having high-status friends. These higher-status peers can exert a positive influence on students, affecting their plans to attend college and their choice of classes and curriculum (Campbell and Alexander 1965; Felmlee and Eder 1983; Alwin and Otto 1977). According to this perspective, students in higher SES context schools have better educational outcomes because they are more likely to have friends with better academic habits and higher aspirations.

The other major explanation of socioeconomic contextual effects focuses on normative climates of schools rather than on interpersonal influences. This view suggests that the socioeconomic composition of a school influences particular normative standards within schools and classrooms, and these, in turn, influence student conduct (see Alexander and Eckland 1975; Rutter et al. 1979; McDill and Rigsby 1973; Campbell and Alexander 1965; Brookover et al. 1979). Because students from higher-status backgrounds tend to have higher aspirations and achievement, as well as more favorable attitudes toward school, they foster the development of general organizational norms that support high achievement. Students' and teachers' beliefs about their schools' academic and behavioral expectations in turn influence educational aspirations and achievement-related behaviors.

*Ability context.* A number of studies have also examined the influence of the "academic ability context" of a school, usually measured by the average ability level of a school's students. Consistent with the literature on tracking discussed below, these studies suggest that, when students are in an environment with other high-achieving students, their own achievement tends to increase (see Bridge et al. 1979; Beckerman and Good 1981). Average ability levels, however, have the *opposite* effect on educational aspirations. In contrast to the findings regarding high socioeconomic contexts, when students' individual characteristics are controlled, attending a school with more students of high ability tends to be related to *lower* educational aspirations and *less* favorable assessments of one's academic ability (Meyer 1970; Nelson 1972; Alexander and Eckland 1975; Felson and Reed 1986; Marsh and Parker 1984; Bachman and O'Malley 1986).

Explanations of this effect note that a student's peers serve as a reference group. Students tend to compare themselves with others with whom they go to school. Those who are surrounded by students with greater ability appear to downgrade their own aspirations and self-appraisals, while those who are surrounded by students of lesser ability tend to upgrade their own aspirations and self-assessments. As James Davis (1966) noted in his work with college students, students look at their own "frog pond" in assessing their self-worth and developing future aspirations. Just as a frog's assessment of his own size depends upon the size of his surroundings, students who are in a relatively small "frog pond," with few peers who are noticeably more capable, tend to develop more favorable self-assessments. In contrast, students with equal ability levels who find themselves surrounded by a number of people with equal and greater ability tend to downgrade their assessments of their own ability.

These results point out how important it may be to consider that the effect of an environmental variable can vary depending upon the dependent variable that is studied. A high-ability context appears to enhance academic achievement but diminish self-appraisals and future aspirations. Although academic achievement is certainly a precursor to successful adult life, it by no means explains all of the variance in later occupational success (see Jencks et al. 1979), and many scholars, especially those writing in the status attainment tradition (e.g., Hauser 1971; Blau and Duncan 1967; Sewell and Shah 1968; Jencks et al. 1979), see academic achievement as an intervening variable in accounting for adult aspirations and eventual occupational status.

It is also important to remember that the nature of a school's ability context and socioeconomic context are highly related. Schools with high socioeconomic levels tend also to be those with high average ability levels. A high socioeconomic context tends to enhance students' aspirations by increasing the probability of associations with high-status peers and the presence of strong academic norms. Through its strong correlation with a high-ability context, however, it can also lower aspirations by decreasing the relative rank at which a person falls within a school. In essence, the effects of the two variables tend to cancel each other out, and their individual effects cannot be determined without introducing the other variable as a control (Alexander and Eckland 1975; Meyer 1970; Nelson 1972). In understanding how students' academic ability affects their assessments and future plans, it is important to consider not just their individual ability levels but also their ranking relative to other students within their school.

The way in which the ability context and socioeconomic context of schools affect students' aspirations and self-assessments may vary across schools with different socioeconomic contexts. Upper-class schools, where both teachers and students are oriented toward preparations for college, may be more likely than other schools to encourage students to compare their abilities with global standards, such as those assessed by national-level tests. In these schools, the depressing effect of a high-ability context may be relatively weak, thus allowing peer influences on aspirations to be greater. This could result in a stronger effect of socioeconomic context on higher aspirations (Meyer 1970). In contrast, in middle-class schools, a student from a lower-status background may develop higher desires for greater education through contacts with peers. Yet the competition within the school and a lessened emphasis on a national comparison group could lead to lower self-assessments. Thus Robert Bain and James Anderson (1974, p. 444) suggest that "the greatest amount of psychological tension or dissonance between a relatively high desire to attend college but a relatively low self-perceived scholastic ability to go to college should be found among lower-class students attending middle-class schools."

*Sex composition.* Federal regulations, especially Title IX of the Education Amendments of 1972, specifically forbid discrimination or exclusion based on sex in any educational program or activity (Williams 1980, pp. 145-46). No doubt reflecting a widespread belief that coeducation is somehow preferable to single-sex education, single-sex colleges and public schools have virtually disappeared in the United States. The major exceptions are a few private, generally Catholic, high schools and colleges. The High School and Beyond data set, a large, national sample of high school students in a wide variety of schools (see Coleman et al. 1982) includes data on a number of both coeducational and single-sex high schools and has been used by researchers to explore the effect of single-sex education on high school students' achievement.

The literature reviewed to this point suggests that most students tend to have higher achievement in more heterogeneous environments: Desegregated schools enhance minority students' achievement, and students also have higher achievement when they are placed with students from higher socioeconomic backgrounds and with higher abilities. In contrast, the data regarding single-sex high schools suggest that many students do better in sex-segregated settings. Girls from all racial and ethnic backgrounds and Hispanic and African American boys appear to have higher achievement gains, higher educational aspirations, better attitudes toward learning, more egalitarian attitudes toward women, and a greater sense of environmental control in single-sex schools than in mixed-sex schools. These results persist even when differences in individual background and ability and school-related variables are statistically controlled. The one exception to this pattern involves boys in the white majority. They tend to do better on these dimensions when they are in mixed-sex schools (Lee and Bryk 1986; Riordan 1990).

Cornelius Riordan (1990, p. 151) suggests that

> single-sex schools offer an environment that is more conducive to learning than mixed-sex schools, especially for women. . . . In all-girl schools, the adolescent climate is weak, allowing an academic climate to flourish. In all-boy schools, the adolescent climate is strong, but it is accompanied by a strong disciplinary structure.

In other words, the single-sex environment allows an academic orientation or climate, which can be more strongly influenced by school policies, to predominate over a peer group climate, which tends to emphasize the development of cross-sex relationships rather than academic success.

## Within-School Groupings and Educational Outcomes

Although the literature reviewed above describes how the composition of a school can affect students' achievement and other educational outcomes, other research has focused on how groupings within schools, such as ability groups and curricular tracks, influence achievement (Meyer 1970; Alexander et al. 1978; Oakes 1985; Vanfossen et al. 1987).

## ABILITY GROUPING

Ability grouping is commonly used in both elementary and secondary schools to reduce the heterogeneity of instructional groups. It involves the teaching of classes or subgroups within classes at different levels for students of different abilities (see Oakes 1985, 1987). Much of the research in this area has not used the most sophisticated randomized experimental designs. Nor has it explored instructional techniques, interactions, and peer influences in ability groups in detail. Yet the findings across studies are fairly consistent. A large number of studies from a wide range of years suggest that, when students are in an environment with other high-achieving students, their own achievement tends to increase. In contrast, ability grouping appears to be detrimental for low-ability students. In other words, although ability grouping may sometimes benefit high-achieving students, a good deal of research indicates that it impedes the progress of students in lower groups (see Bridge et al. 1979; Kulik and Kulik 1982, 1984; Esposito 1973; Begle 1975; Brophy and Good 1986; Hallinan 1987, 1990; Sorensen and Hallinan 1986). In addition, ability grouping can affect status differences in a classroom, with those in lower groups held in lower esteem (Hallinan 1984). Thus ability grouping can actually lead to larger differences between the high and low ends of the achievement and social distribution within a school or classroom.

In general, different types of grouping systems may have different effects on learning outcomes. For instance, some studies suggest that various types of ability groupings can sometimes benefit students in mathematics classes (Slavin and Karweit 1985; Dewar 1964; Smith 1960). Other work suggests that the Joplin plan, which calls for cross-grade grouping of students in reading and whole-class instruction (Moorhouse 1964; Kierstad 1963; Skapski 1960), can enhance achievement (Slavin 1987a, 1987b, 1990b).

It is important to remember that research on ability grouping can involve intense debates about the exact nature of its effects (see, for example, Slavin 1990a, 1990b; Hallinan 1990), and the research has often been criticized for methodological shortcomings (Sorensen and Hallinan 1986; Sorensen 1970; Filby et al. 1982). Yet various participants in these debates tend to agree that ability grouping does not enhance achievement for the majority of children. In addition, they tend to agree that grouping arrangements that enhance achievement appear to alter the allocation of both instructional and learning time and instructional activities (see Slavin 1987, 1990a, 1990b; Hallinan 1990; Provus 1960; Morris 1969). In other words, as we discuss in more detail below, differential effects in ability-grouped classes appear primarily because the instructional process is altered (see Barr and Dreeben 1983; Gamoran 1986; Hallinan 1990).

Although students' placement in ability groups is associated with their socioeconomic status and race and ethnicity, studies of teachers' placement decisions have failed to uncover racial bias in their assignments (Haller 1985). Instead, variables such as the size of the class, the ability range of the students, and the instructional time available influence the number of groups that a teacher will use and the assignment of children to a particular group. Within these parameters, some researchers have found that teachers will vary the numbers of groups that they use, opting for more groups in larger, more heterogeneous classes with more low-ability children (Barr and Dreeben 1983). Others, however, note that, given the reality of limited instructional time and norms regarding equal attention to all students, teachers tend to have a set number of groups regardless of the heterogeneity of a class (e.g., Hallinan and Sorensen 1983; Hallinan 1984).

As with analyses of other grouping criteria, the explanations of why ability grouping does not enhance achievement, especially among low-achieving students, focus on differences in instructional style and normative climates across peer groups. In general, students in lower-ability groups are more likely to spend time off-task, even when variables such as their individual ability and achievement are controlled. This suggests that both students and teachers tolerate and expect more off-task behavior and inattention in low-ability groups (Felmlee and Eder 1983; Hallinan 1984, p. 232). Given this situation, teachers in low-ability groups must spend more time dealing with administrative and disciplinary matters and less time in active instruction. Evidence also suggests that teachers in low-ability groups use less interesting and challenging materials, proceed at a slower pace, spend less time in preparation, and use poorer teaching skills than with high-ability groups. Students placed in high-ability groups are exposed to the most challenging material, which is presented at the fastest pace, and thus can learn the most in a given time period (Hallinan 1984, 1987; Sorensen and Hallinan 1986; Barr and Dreeben 1983; Gamoran 1986; Rowan and Miracle 1983; Meyer 1980; Filby and Barnett 1982; Eder 1983).

Dreeben and Barr (1988) stress that the different learning outcomes that occur as a result of ability group placement reflect the allocation and mobilization of educational resources and are not simply the result of normative influences or instructional processes internal to the group. In other words, teachers and other school officials can choose who they select for groups and how they allocate and mobilize instructional resources. These decisions, which are made within the organizational context of schools, are the mechanisms by which the effects of ability grouping come about. Maureen Hallinan (1987) suggests that teachers could increase the time they devote to low-ability groups, use more challenging and engaging methods with these students, adjust expectations for these pupils with new information, be more flexible in moving students from one group to another, and try to counteract negative peer influences in lower-ability groups through various reward mechanisms and smaller group size. If they were to adopt these strategies, the negative effects of ability grouping might be lessened.

## TRACKING AND ACHIEVEMENT

Tracking is commonly found in secondary schools and involves the assignment of students to different sequences of courses depending upon their future goals. Typically, one track is designated for college preparatory students, another for general students, and a third for vocational students. Researchers have examined the extent to which tracking enhances students' academic achievement and the extent to which it reinforces social class differences between students within a school.

A very large body of literature indicates that curriculum tracking is related to verbal, mathematics, and science achievement (Bowles 1969; Michelson 1970; Alexander and McDill 1976; Gamoran 1987; Garet and DeLany 1988), educational aspirations (Alexander and McDill 1976; Heyns 1974; Rosenbaum 1980; Vanfossen et al. 1987), self-esteem, attitudes about schoolwork (Bridge et al. 1979; Oakes 1985; Kelly 1975), misbehavior (Schaefer and Olexa 1971), college grades, and the probability that students will drop out of high school and college (Peng et al. 1977; Natriello et al. 1989; Schaefer and Olexa 1971). Although some tracking systems may provide academic advantages for students in the top tracks, the evidence consistently indicates negative results for those in the lower groups. School officials have assumed that, by preventing extensive contact of lower-ability students with their higher-ability peers, the self-esteem and self-concepts of lower-ability students are protected. In fact, exactly the opposite result seems to occur. Instead of feeling more comfortable about themselves, students in lower tracks tend to develop lower self-esteem, lower aspirations, and more negative attitudes toward school (Oakes 1985, 1987).

It is also important to note that the result of higher track placement is not uniformly good. It may enhance achievement but not necessarily increase aspirations or self-evaluations. Students in higher tracks tend to have peers who perform well, thus enhancing group norms regarding performance. Yet, as we noted in our discussion of the ability context of schools, a higher-ability context can lead individuals to give more negative evaluations of their own ability than they would in other contexts. Students compare themselves with others with whom they go to school. Given students of equal ability, those who are surrounded by students with greater ability might tend to downgrade their own aspirations while those who are surrounded by students of lesser ability might tend to upgrade their aspirations (Felson and Reed 1986).

Schools may differ in the extent to which they track students and in the extent to which placement in higher tracks is a relatively exclusive or inclusive phenomenon (Kilgore 1991). Ideally, track placement would only reflect a student's academic achievement, ability, and motivation. In reality, most studies conclude that students' track placements are related to both their prior academic achievement and their social class background (Sorensen 1987), although schools appear to vary in the extent to which socioeconomic status has an influence independent of academic variables (see Jencks et al. 1972; Alexander and Cook 1982; Davis and Haller 1981). For instance, schools that offer students multiple track experiences and have a large number of high SES students might be less likely to have a strong association of social class with track placement than would more heterogeneous, rigidly tracked schools (Alexander and Cook 1982; Hallinan 1990; also Vanfossen et al. 1987).

Many scholars suggest that tracking in secondary schools and ability grouping, its counterpart in elementary schools, function as the mediating variable between students' socioeconomic background and their educational achievement, occupational aspirations, and perceptions of themselves and their school (see Vanfossen et al. 1987; Lee and Bryk 1988; Alexander et al. 1978). These studies suggest that tracking reproduces class status by sorting students from different socioeconomic backgrounds into different curricula and providing them with unequal learning environments. These are reflected both in the normative climates in which they learn and in the quality of instruction they receive (Oakes 1985; Schaefer and Olexa 1971; Alexander and McDill 1976; Barr and Dreeben 1983; Dreeben and Gamoran 1986; Garet and DeLany 1988; Sorensen 1987). In general, these studies suggest that students from lower socioeconomic backgrounds receive educational experiences that offer them limited access to high-status knowledge and normative climates that are not conducive to achievement. In contrast, students from higher socioeconomic backgrounds are much more likely to enroll in challenging curricular programs and college preparatory tracks that provide the type of knowledge and normative standards that are essential for higher levels of education and entrance into high-status occupations. Thus these scholars suggest that tracking helps perpetuate social class inequalities by placing students in distinct learning environments.

Recent research on tracking has tried to identify how tracking effects occur. Quantitative work in this area has shown that differential course-taking patterns, instructional approaches, and student perceptions of teachers account for much of the variation in achievement between students in different tracks as well as differences in educational and occupational aspirations and social-psychological variables such as self-esteem, attitudes about school, and commitment to academic goals (Gamoran and Berends 1987; Gamoran 1987; Alexander and Cook 1982; Lee and Bryk 1988, 1989; Vanfossen et al. 1987).

Ethnographic studies support these conclusions (see Gamoran and Berends 1987; Ball 1981; Gamoran 1986; Metz 1986; Finley 1984; Oakes 1985; Rosenbaum 1976; Eckert 1989). Extensive observations suggest that school tracks differ in instructional practices and normative climates. For instance, variations in instruction, such as pace, complexity, and quality, and the allocation of experienced versus nonexperienced teachers favor high-track classes. Similarly, variations in teacher and student interactions, attitudes, and perceptions of themselves, each other, and their school favor high-track classes. Teachers tend to view high-track students more positively, and high-track students tend to choose friends with similar academic standing, form cohesive cliques, and support and help each other more in their class work (Finley 1984; Rosenbaum 1976; Oakes 1985). Track placement is also related to variations in the expectations students and teachers hold about educational outcomes. High-track classes are given more value by both teachers and students. Students in those tracks receive more encouragement and, in turn, increase their efforts in school, are less disruptive, and are less alienated from school (Rosenbaum 1976; Oakes 1985; Metz 1978; Finley 1984). In sum, the evidence consistently indicates that high-track students obtain greater educational advantages than their low-track counterparts.

The net effect of tracking is long term. Mobility between tracks can occur but is more often downward than upward. In addition, given the negative effects of lower-track placement, the chance of a student in such a placement ever catching up to the point where he or she could enter a more rapidly advancing higher track is quite small. School officials often justify and promote tracking policies because they believe that they are in the best interest of students. The evidence appears to suggest the contrary.

## Summary and Implications

The literature reviewed in this chapter fairly consistently demonstrates that greater learning takes place in heterogeneous settings. Minority students perform better when they are in desegregated schools, especially beginning in the early grades. Students also show higher achievement in settings with more high-ability and high-status students and when they are not tracked into lower curricular areas or low-ability groups. These results hold even when individual variables such as socioeconomic status or measured ability are held constant. Three exceptions to these patterns are notable: First, students may have enhanced achievement in high-ability contexts, but their self-evaluations and aspirations may be somewhat lower when they are surrounded by high-ability and high-achieving peers. Second, girls from all types of backgrounds and boys from racial and ethnic minorities appear to have higher achievement when they are in single-sex secondary schools, which are more homogeneous environments, rather than in mixed-sex schools. Third, although practices of tracking and ability grouping do not generally appear to benefit students from lower-status backgrounds and/or lower achievement levels, they may benefit higher-status, higher-ability, and higher-achieving students. Similarly, white boys benefit more from mixed-sex secondary schools than from single-sex schools.

Explanations for these effects focus on differential instructional practices and group norms and expectations in learning groups. Teachers appear to cover material more quickly, to hold higher expectations, and to teach more effectively in higher-track and higher-ability groups than in other groups. In addition, both students and teachers are more likely to hold higher academic expectations, to expect better behavior, and to devote more time to academic learning in the higher tracks and ability groups. Girls and minority boys in single-sex secondary schools are less distracted by elements of the peer culture and also devote themselves more wholeheartedly to academic endeavors. Within the more heterogeneous settings, students seem to develop different ideas of what they can do; they develop a better locus of control. They may develop higher expectations of themselves than they would have in other groups and thus alter their behavior in ways that help accomplish these expectations.

It should be noted that current practices in schools are far from the most optimal, at least as suggested by this literature. Many minority children attend segregated schools, especially in the early grades, when desegregation is so important. Schools also remain highly differentiated by social status and ability level, and within-school tracking and ability grouping are very common. Within schools that are desegregated, tracking and ability grouping often occur and work against the benefits that could accrue from the desegregated school environment. Although generally prompted by the good intentions of educators, these practices simply exacerbate already existing differences in status and achievement and serve to perpetuate social class differences. The net effect of these various grouping practices is long term, as children in lower tracks and ability groups or in segregated schools fall progressively behind their same-age peers. The chances of catching up are slim.

These grouping practices can be changed by school policy. Many experts now urge teachers to consider cross-ability grouping and forms of cooperative learning within the classroom. Meta-analyses of studies of cooperative learning assert that these practices promote achievement that is at least as high and often higher than that in traditional classrooms. It also appears to promote "positive interpersonal relations, motivation to learn, and self-esteem among students" (Bossert 1988a, p. 225; see also Wilkinson 1988; Slavin 1990c). We will return to these issues in Chapter 6, when we discuss policy issues in more detail. In the next chapter, we look more closely at the normative climates of schools and examine their impact on student outcomes and educational experiences.

# 2

# School and Classroom Climates

The literature reviewed in Chapter 1 suggests that the composition of the groups in which students learn can affect their achievement. Such a contextual analysis, however, can only give a partial picture of the influences on student learning, for measures of the ability, social class, or racial composition of a school are only proxies or indirect measures of learning-related norms (see McDill et al. 1967). To more fully understand how schools facilitate higher achievement, we also need to look directly at the relationships between students and teachers and the attitudes, norms, and values that characterize schools and classrooms (see Entwisle and Hayduk 1982; Goodlad 1984).

Fortunately, a large number of researchers have attempted this task by trying to describe how the overall "climate" or "culture" of a school affects learning. Although they have used a wide variety of approaches, they generally base their work on the premise that schools are social organizations and, as such, provide a context in which students and other school personnel interact. Moreover, whatever method these researchers have used, the results have been relatively consistent. Schools and classrooms that enhance achievement appear to be characterized by high academic expectations, effective leadership, an orderly atmosphere, and warmth, concern, and respect for others. Below, we first describe the wide variety of work in this area. We then move to a summary of research on effective schools and classrooms.

Although we discuss school and classroom environments separately below, it should be noted that they are not mutually exclusive. Understanding school climates necessarily includes an understanding of classroom-level interactions, although research that focuses on classrooms often notes the significance of schoolwide influences, such as the leadership style of the principal or distributions of resources (see Tornatzky et al. 1980). Clearly, school and classroom environments are intertwined, and a holistic portrait of how schools can enhance achievement can only emerge when researchers remain sensitive to how various organizational levels are interrelated. (For exemplary research of this nature, see Lightfoot 1983; Metz 1986; Goodlad 1984.) We use the school/classroom dichotomy in this chapter primarily as an organizational device and do not mean to obscure the linkage between the two environments. (See Fraser et al. 1987 and Fraser and Rentoul 1982 for work that incorporates both classroom and school climate measures.)

## Describing School Environments

Researchers have used a variety of approaches in developing holistic pictures of school environments. Some use the insights of organizational psychologists and social psychologists to develop standardized measures of school climate and school health. Others, inspired by work of anthropologists and ethnographers, use a more global and qualitative notion of school culture. Still others take a more empirical and applied approach and simply try to describe the characteristics of schools that are unusually effective. All of these researchers, however, have been concerned with developing overall pictures or portraits of the unique characteristics of schools as social organizations and how these characteristics can help enhance achievement.

### SCHOOL CLIMATES

Underlying the notion of school or organizational climates is the view that organizations or groups have their own personalities, much as individuals do (see Moos 1976, 1979; Halpin and Croft 1962; Halpin 1966; Hoy et al. 1991; Pace and Stern 1958). Tagiuri (1968) is often cited as providing a useful definition of organizational climate (e.g., Anderson 1982; Miskel and Ogawa 1988), suggesting that it involves four dimensions: *ecology,* the physical environment in which a group interacts; *milieu,* the social characteristics of individuals and groups participating in the organizations; *social system*, the patterned relationships of persons and groups; and *culture*, the collectively accepted beliefs, values, and meanings of the group. Wayne Hoy and his colleagues (1991, p. 10) provide a more succinct definition: "School climate is the relatively enduring quality of the school environment that is experienced by participants, affects their behavior, and is based on their collective perception of behavior in schools." A large number of researchers suggest that this notion of climate can help link characteristics of organizations with individuals' attitudes and behaviors and show how organizations affect individuals' behavior independently of their own characteristics. In other words, the same individual may behave quite differently in groups with different organizational climates (see Field and Abelson 1982; Hellriegel and Slocum 1974; Tagiuri and Litwin 1968; Campbell et al. 1970; Forehand and Gilmer 1964; Jones and James 1979; Schneider 1975; Schneider and Reichers 1983; Anderson 1982; Bidwell and Kasarda 1975; Moos 1979; Bidwell 1965).

Researchers have typically measured organizational climate by assessing group members' perceptions of organizational characteristics. One of the earliest examples is Pace and Stern's (1958) attempt to describe college students' and faculty members' perceptions of their environments. Their work served as a model for a great deal of later research by showing how scholars could use standardized scales to measure individuals' perceptions of their environment and that group members tend to agree about the characteristics of their group. Halpin and Croft (1962; Halpin 1966; see also Hoy et al. 1991) are generally cited as the first to develop measures of a school's climate. They developed a series of 64 items that teachers and principals could use to describe the climate of their schools and found substantial agreement within a given school on the nature of its climate. Through various statistical manipulations, they developed ways to characterize schools on a variety of descriptive dimensions, such as the extent of collegial teacher behavior and supportive behaviors of the principal.

Later work has followed in this mode, using the perceptions of teachers, principals, and sometimes students to assess the nature of a school's or classroom's climate (see Miskel and Ogawa 1988; Hoy et al. 1991; McDill et al. 1967; Willower et al. 1967). The results of this work consistently support the intuitive view that schools and classrooms differ in their climate or personalities and that participants in these settings generally agree to a great extent in the way they perceive these characteristics. The results also demonstrate that these differences can be described with quantifiable data and linked with school outcomes such as achievement. Researchers in this tradition suggest that such measures can be of special use to those who are interested in describing behaviors in schools and managing and changing them in ways that are more effective (see Hoy et al. 1991, p. 7).

## SCHOOL CULTURES

The notion of school culture is used like that of school climate to capture the feelings and nature of an organization. Hoy and his associates (1991, p. 5) suggest that organizational culture may be defined as "a system of shared orientations that hold the unit together and give it a distinctive identity." This may involve the shared norms, values, ideologies, and taken-for-granted assumptions within a group (see Hoy et al. 1991, pp. 5-7; Schein 1990). Although those who study organizational climates tend to be influenced by work in psychology and social psychology and primarily employ quantitative, survey methodologies, those who study organizational cultures tend to be influenced more by anthropology and sociology and to use more qualitative ethnographic techniques of intensive interviews and observations.

It is perhaps not surprising that researchers who focus their work on either climates or cultures may sometimes speak past each other. Tagiuri's definition of *climate* presented above includes the notion of culture, including a group's values, beliefs, and meanings, as simply one aspect, implying that the concept of climate is more broad reaching than that of culture. Those who study organizational cultures take an opposite view, suggesting that "climate is only a surface manifestation of culture" (Schein 1990, p. 109). Although those who measure school climates are generally interested in how climates affect achievement, those who study school and classroom cultures are often just as, if not more, interested in how these cultures develop. These are definitional disputes, no doubt reflecting the disciplinary roots of the two lines of research, and they cannot be resolved empirically. Instead, the results of both types of studies can complement each other; and, in fact, the results from studies of school and classroom cultures are generally strikingly similar to those of school climates. We use both types of studies in our later review of the empirical literature but tend to use the word *climate* somewhat more, reflecting its predominance in the literature.

## RESEARCH ON EFFECTIVE SCHOOLS

The final group of research that focuses on the totality of school environments tends to be relatively atheoretical. These researchers look at "school effectiveness," trying to identify the attributes and characteristics that distinguish "effective" schools and "effective" teachers from their less effective counterparts (see Purkey and Smith 1982; Good and Brophy 1986). This research has generally defined effective schools as those that "promote the average academic achievement" of their students (Good and Brophy 1986, p. 570) and has involved both qualitative and quantitative examinations of school and classroom characteristics (e.g., Klitgaard and Hall 1973; Weber 1971; Brookover et al. 1979; Rutter et al. 1979). This work clearly shows that, when student background and prior achievement are controlled, certain school and classroom environments can generate higher achievement (Armor et al. 1976; Murnane 1975).

Much of this research has focused on schools comprising students from disadvantaged backgrounds—the groups most likely to experience achievement problems. This has the effect of essentially controlling for the influence of the socioeconomic context of a school on achievement by limiting the variability of this variable. This practice, however, also limits the potential generalizability of findings to other types of schools. In general, work in this tradition tends to be somewhat atheoretical in nature, somewhat limited in generalizability, and often methodologically unsophisticated, looking only at schools or even districts as the unit of analysis. Yet this "school effectiveness" literature has produced results that parallel those from studies of school culture and school climate as well as those conducted with the individual student as the unit of analysis or those using complicated multilevel analyses. Thus these effectiveness studies are also included in our review.

## Effective School Environments

Nearly four decades of research have contributed to our current portrait of effective learning environments. It must be remembered that research in this area is still continuing, and new results and understandings will continue to emerge for many years. Nevertheless, despite the different disciplinary roots and sometimes various goals of this research, the results are fairly consistent. In general, the impact of school-level variables on school climate and student achievement can be seen as involving four broad areas: (a) academic expectations and excellence; (b) strong, collaborative school leadership; (c) orderly environments and school coherence; and (d) high student and teacher morale. These all appear to involve, in a very general sense, the norms and common values that promote learning within a school and the nature of relationships among school members.

### ACADEMIC EXPECTATIONS AND EXCELLENCE

A large number of studies demonstrate that schools in which both students and staff value academic excellence tend to have higher levels of academic achievement. For instance, from their extensive work with secondary students, Edward McDill and his associates (McDill et al. 1967; McDill and Rigsby 1973; McDill et al. 1969) suggest that schools that teachers and students see as emphasizing intellectualism, subject matter competency, and a commitment to academic excellence are more likely to have higher levels of mathematics achievement and higher levels of educational aspirations. These climate variables significantly influence students even when individual attributes, such as their socioeconomic background, ability, academic values, and the socioeconomic context of their schools, are controlled.

The relationship between high academic expectations among students and staff and high achievement has been supported in work with both elementary and secondary students, case studies of schools (Brookover and Lezotte 1979; Phi Delta Kappa 1980; Weber 1971; Cookson and Persell 1985), survey studies (Brookover and Schneider 1975; Lipsitz 1984; Schneider et al. 1979; Hoy et al. 1991), longitudinal studies (Rutter et al. 1979), and work using the large High School and Beyond data set (Coleman et al. 1982; Hoffer et al. 1987; Greeley 1982). For instance, Sarah Lightfoot's (1983) extensive ethnographic work suggests that high-achieving secondary schools are those where the staff are concerned with the rationale, coherence, and integrity of the curriculum and are committed to academic pursuits. Similarly, using survey methods, McDill and Rigsby (1973) suggest that schools that offer students either the opportunity for advanced placement or the opportunity to participate in an accelerated curriculum demonstrate a commitment to academic excellence and, in turn, nurture that commitment in students and faculty. Wilbur Brookover and his associates, in their studies of elementary schools, report that school members' attitudes are related to increasing levels of school achievement. Most important among these are staff commitment to improving students' academic performance; high and/or increasing expectations of teachers about students, such as high opinions of student abilities; peer norms emphasizing academics; and staff insistence on reaching basic reading and math goals (Brookover et al. 1978, 1979; Brookover and Lezotte 1979; Brookover and Schneider 1975). High staff and student expectations appear to lower a student's "sense of futility" and construct the impression that teachers do care and students can succeed (see also Phi Delta Kappa 1980). In general, these studies consistently tend to indicate that schools with teachers and students who see higher achievement as a real and attainable goal actually do have higher achievement.

Other studies indicate that, in addition to valuing and expecting academic excellence, frequent and public rewards and praise for academic accomplishments and good behavior help create a positive learning climate (Brookover et al. 1979; Rutter et al. 1979; Wynne 1980). Mary Metz (1986), however, suggests that, if the learning climate of the *school* is to be enhanced, rewards and praise need to be based on students' individual progress rather than on the comparison of students with each other.

Finally, some forms of academic competition may enhance student outcomes. Group, rather than individual, competition can promote student camaraderie, which boosts school spirit and contributes to greater achievement by promoting positive perceptions about school (Brookover et al. 1979; Wynne 1980). Technological and academic arrangements that offer students the opportunity to cooperate with each other in groups and only permit competition between groups can also help promote academic work and positive learning environments (Metz 1978). Perhaps individual competition differentiates students from each other and contributes to negative perceptions of the learning environment among students who do not succeed as well as others. Competition between heterogeneous groups, on the other hand, may obscure individual performance, promote cooperation among students of various abilities, and nurture a positive perception among all students (see Slavin 1990c; Bossert 1988a; Coleman and Hoffer 1986, pp. 237-38).

## SCHOOL LEADERSHIP

A second important dimension of effective school environments appears to be strong, administrative leadership, a variable most often noted in the school effectiveness literature (e.g., Brookover and Lezotte 1979; Edmonds 1979a, 1979b; Klitgaard and Hall 1973; Purkey and Smith 1982; Levine 1990; Fullan 1990). Although these studies do not argue that this is the only factor that accounts for a school's effectiveness, they suggest that, in "effective" or "improving" schools, the principal is perceived as a strong leader, as having control over school functions, and as an expert instructional manager. Especially effective principals appear to be those who are involved in instruction (Brookover et al. 1979; Brookover and Lezotte 1979; Edmonds 1979a, 1979b;

Teddlie et al. 1989; Young 1980; Levine 1990; McLaughlin and Talbert 1990), communicate high expectations for staff members (Brookover et al. 1979; Brookover and Lezotte 1979; Phi Delta Kappa 1980; Levine 1990), promote good feelings and collegiality between faculty and administrators and among faculty (Ellett and Walberg 1979; Levine 1990; Lightfoot 1983; McLaughlin and Talbert 1990), and encourage teacher participation in the school's decision-making processes (Ellett and Walberg 1979; Rutter et al. 1979; Levine 1990).

Effective administrators promote both academic learning and cohesive relations within a school; they perform a balancing act, with a high concern for both task accomplishments and cohesive social relations. Effective principals seem to promote higher achievement by actively encouraging high expectations for students and promoting teaching situations that allow the most effective and extensive instructional contacts. This involves not just efficient scheduling and management but also the development of an ethos or culture that enhances morale, mutual trust and respect, and shared norms and values (Good and Brophy 1986, p. 596; Cohen 1983; Grant 1982; Halpin 1966, p. 170; Hoy et al. 1991, pp. 139, 150; Bossert 1988b, p. 346).

It is probably impossible to provide a single image of a school leader that would be appropriate for all schools. Much of the early work in the school climate tradition was oriented toward facilitating better matches between school climates and leadership styles of potential administrations and suggests that the congruence or "fit" between the perceptions and orientations of various members of a school is important in defining a school's climate (Halpin 1966; Halpin and Croft 1962; Hoy et al. 1991). Other strands of research rely on case studies and ethnographic accounts of a school's culture. This work suggests that effective leadership techniques depend upon pressures imposed by district administrators, the local community, students' needs, and the personal beliefs and experiences of the principal and other members of the school's staff (Bossert et al. 1982; Dwyer 1984; Rowan 1983; Levine 1990). An "effective" leadership style emerges out of an understanding of the impact these factors have on the internal life of schools. Moreover, changes at the administrative level within a school are generally not sufficient to promote long-term changes in student achievement. School boards, district administrators, staff, and students all help create school climates and cultures, and the techniques principals use to enhance achievement may not be effective unless the organizational goals they seek are consistent with the educational values of other school participants (see also Willower 1977; Levine 1990).

Although this research shuns simplistic suggestions for cultivating effective leadership styles, it tends to favor a human relations approach. The effective principal is portrayed as one who creates an environment that emphasizes achievement and intellectualism; nurtures cooperative relationships among school members; offers staff members help, support, and recognition; develops a sense of collegiality with the faculty; and allots staff and students maximum participation in the decision-making process (Dwyer 1984; Ellett and Walberg 1979; Newmann et al. 1989; Owens and Steinhoff 1989; Rutter et al. 1979; Metz 1978). In short, an effective leader is portrayed as one who creatively balances both the organizational and the relational processes of a school (see also Firestone and Wilson 1983; Willower 1977; Wimpelberg 1986). It is interesting to note, in Lightfoot's (1983) ethnographic description *The Good High School*, that effective school principals were those who exhibited qualities of nurturance, receptivity, and responsiveness to relationships and context—qualities traditionally defined as "feminine" (see also Levine 1990, p. 582). Effective principals seem able to enhance both instrumental goal attainment and collegial, supportive relationships among all school members.

## ORDERLY ENVIRONMENTS AND SCHOOL COHERENCE

A third important element of effective school environments is an atmosphere that is orderly without being rigid (Edmonds 1979a, 1979b), one that maintains a consistent set of rules and values that clearly map out school goals and policies (Phi Delta Kappa 1980; Rutter et al. 1979) while also promoting "purposefulness and pleasure in learning" (Weber 1971). Such an atmosphere appears to enhance students' learning as well as cohesive relationships among school members (Levine 1990; Perrone et al. 1985; McLaughlin and Talbert 1990).

An orderly environment appears to affect achievement in a variety of ways. First, it provides a disciplinary climate within which students' and teachers' opportunities to conduct task-related work are maximized (Coleman 1982; Peng et al. 1982; Hoffer et al. 1987; Greeley 1982). Second, an orderly and purposeful atmosphere promotes a sense of efficacy among teachers and students, which, in turn, enhances teaching and learning performances (Metz 1986; Newmann et al. 1989). Third, simply the consistency and stability associated with an orderly environment appears to promote higher achievement (McDill and Rigsby 1973; Newmann et al. 1989; Phi Delta Kappa 1980; Rutter et al. 1979; Silberman 1970).

This effect of a stable and consistent environment appears strongest in schools where both faculty and students more often participate in decision-making processes and other activities. This higher level of involvement appears to enhance shared norms and values, which, in turn, help create positive relationships among all school members (Rutter et al. 1979; Wynne 1980; Mitchell 1967; Breckenridge 1976; Ellett and Walberg 1979; Urich and Batchelder 1979). Shared activities by staff and students, ample opportunities for students to participate in school activities, and staff and student participation in decision making might help promote a belief by students and staff that the norms and disciplinary practices of a school are fair. This perception appears to be highly related to both orderly school environments and higher achievement (Coleman et al. 1982). In general, an orderly and coherent school environment appears to promote student achievement by enhancing collegial relationships and promoting an atmosphere of trust, caring, and cooperation (see Chubb 1988; Lightfoot 1983; Metz 1978, 1986).

## TEACHER AND STUDENT MORALE

School members' perceptions and attitudes about their environment are the fourth important dimension of school environments. Teachers who report satisfaction with their work setting are more likely to express high morale and perceive the school's climate as open and supportive of their role (Kalis 1980; Newmann et al. 1989; Sargeant 1967). In turn, students who perceive their teachers as satisfied with their jobs are more likely to exhibit high levels of attendance and achievement (Brookover and Lezotte 1979), high morale about their learning environment, and more academic self-confidence (Edmonds 1979a; Schneider et al. 1979; Weber 1971). Schools that can nurture high morale among students and staff seem to maximize their chances of developing attitudes about individual abilities as well as a learning environment that promote higher levels of achievement (see also Lightfoot 1983; Coleman et al. 1982; Perrone et al. 1985; Levine 1990; Fullan 1990; Mortimore et al. 1988; Corcoran 1990; Goodlad 1984).

In her study of three magnet schools, Mary Metz (1986) shows how teacher morale influences students' learning. She found that, through their shared involvement and satisfaction with their work, their shared "pride of craft," the faculty helps promote a positive or healthy school climate, which then promotes higher student achievement. Unfortunately, Metz suggests that this finding may only be valid for schools that do not cater to low-achieving students. Working with low-achieving students can have a devastating effect on teachers who have a strong sense of occupational pride and efficacy. Teachers who express a great deal of pride and satisfaction in their work appear to be most effective in classrooms where actual student achievement provides support for their sense of satisfaction. Other studies suggest that teachers communicate their sense of pride to students in all their verbal and nonverbal interactions. This establishes a "circle of causation." Students' achievements influence teachers' morale, sense of efficacy, and expectations for students, which, in turn, directly influence higher levels of student achievement (Ashton and Webb 1986; Chubb 1988; Newmann et al. 1989; Rosenholtz 1985).

## Effective Classroom Environments

Students actually spend most of their school time within classrooms, and thus it is important to directly study these environments. A good deal of work suggests that classroom environments are very important in influencing students' attitudes toward school as well as their achievement, and that the classroom environment can mediate between more macro-level influences, such as the school and community, and individual student outcomes (Armor et al. 1976; Cronbach and Snow 1977; Murnane 1975; Moos 1979; O'Reilly 1975; Walberg 1969a, 1969b; Cohen et al. 1989).

Much of our knowledge of effective teaching and classrooms comes from the tradition of "process-product" research. This work focuses directly on how the instructional behaviors of teachers affect students' learning and has been instrumental in improving teachers' day-to-day pedagogical practices (see Rosenshine 1971; Centra and Potter 1980; Dunkin and Biddle 1974; Puff 1978; Fraser 1986; Brophy and Good 1986, for reviews). The other major source of work in this area comes from the "socioecological" studies of classroom climate, which examine the relationship of students' achievement to their perceptions of their classrooms. This research is rapidly expanding and is far from conclusive. In general, however, the research suggests that classroom variables that influence student achievement parallel those noted for schools: the achievement-related expectations and values of students and teachers, the role of the teacher (as contrasted to the principal in the school-level analysis) as an effective instructor, an orderly atmosphere conducive to learning, and high student and teacher morale. These findings are noted both in the somewhat atheoretical, descriptive accounts of variables that distinguish "effective classrooms" and describe effective teaching methods as well as in the more theoretically oriented studies of classroom climate and cultures.

## EFFECTIVE TEACHING

Most of the conclusions regarding the linkages between teachers' behaviors and students' achievement have been widely replicated. Although they may vary somewhat when children of different grade levels or different backgrounds are studied or with different subject areas, the pattern of results remains largely consistent (Brophy and Good 1986, p. 360). Similar results appear with urban, rural, and suburban schools and with both quantitative and observational data (Teddlie et al. 1989). In general, the literature suggests that the quantity and pacing of instruction, the way in which teachers give information, the way in which teachers question students and wait for responses, and the way they handle seat work and homework all influence student achievement (Puff 1978; Klitgaard and Hall 1973; Rutter et al. 1979; Austin 1979; Mortimore et al. 1988; Brophy and Good 1986; Rosenshine 1983; Teddlie et al. 1989).

The findings regarding the quantity and pacing of instruction have been most consistently replicated. As would be intuitively expected, students have higher achievement when more of the curriculum is covered and when more time is spent actively engaged in learning that is appropriate to their level. This is most likely to occur when teachers see academic instruction as a major part of their role and when they are effective classroom managers, maintaining an orderly environment that maximizes children's opportunities to learn. Effective classroom managers seem able to monitor the entire class continuously, do two things simultaneously without having to break the flow of classroom events, move activities along at a good pace without confusion or loss of focus, and provide work that is at the right level of difficulty for students and is interesting enough to hold their attention. The most effective teachers are able to balance an inherent tension between covering as much material as possible and ensuring that their students are mastering the material without being either frustrated or bored. In general, students seem to learn most where teachers are actively involved in teaching or supervising their students rather than relying on curriculum materials to relay the content. (See Kounin 1970; Brophy 1979; Brophy and Good 1986; Brophy and Evertson 1976; Good 1979; Rosenshine 1979; Stallings et al. 1978; Stringfield et al. 1985; Anderson 1982; Teddlie et al. 1989; Fisher and Berliner 1985; Berliner 1979; Carroll 1963; Rosenshine and Berliner 1976; Gettinger 1989; Cohen et al. 1989; Leechor 1988, as examples of work related to this area.)

The way in which teachers present information also affects achievement. In general, well-organized and structured presentations help students organize and remember material. Achievement is also enhanced when key concepts and general rules are repeated, when presentations are as clear as possible, and, especially for older students, when teachers are enthusiastic about the subject matter (Brophy and Good 1986, p. 362). Teachers may structure their questions for students in ways that are most likely to enhance achievement by carefully considering the difficulty and cognitive level of the content and by skillfully eliciting responses and reacting to students' answers and comments. Similarly, seat work and homework can be structured in ways that are more likely to reinforce students' learning rather than simply being busywork (see Brophy and Good 1986 for summaries of this work).

## EFFECTIVE CLIMATES

Studies from the socioecological tradition of studying classroom climate support findings from the process-product tradition by suggesting that effective classrooms appear to promote positive relationships among classroom members and have procedures oriented toward academic success. Researchers in this tradition are not primarily interested in describing the characteristics of effective schools or classrooms but in how children's perceptions of their learning environments affect both cognitive and affective development (Moos 1979; O'Reilly 1975; Walberg 1969a, 1969b; Walberg and Anderson 1968, 1972). (See Fraser 1986 for an extensive discussion of measures of classroom climate.)

Herbert Walberg and his associates (Walberg 1969, 1979; Walberg and Anderson 1968, 1972) conceptualize classroom climate as involving both a structural and an affective dimension. The structural dimension refers to the organization of student roles within the class, role expectations, and shared, group-sanctioned behavior or norms. The affective dimension refers to the unique ways in which individual personality needs are satisfied. Both aspects appear to affect student learning.

Research on classroom climate has explored the relationship of students' perceptions of their environment to individual learning (Walberg and Anderson 1968; Anderson 1970), differential class performance (Anderson and Walberg 1968), and academic achievement (O'Reilly 1975; Walberg 1975; Walberg and Anderson 1972). The results obtained in these studies have been very consistent. For example, classes perceived by students as difficult, satisfying, and without friction, apathy, or cliques gain more than those without these characteristics in physics, general science, and mathematics achievement as well as in science interest and activities (Walberg 1969a; Walberg and Anderson 1968, 1972; O'Reilly 1975). Extensive meta-analyses of a wide variety of studies in this area show that students' perceptions of classroom environments can account for a good deal of the variation in students' achievement (Fraser 1986, citing Anderson and Walberg 1972; Haertel et al. 1981).

Some research also indicates that the congruence between students' preferred classroom environment and their actual classroom environment may be just as important as the actual nature of the classroom environment in predicting achievement. This could suggest that certain achievement outcomes might be enhanced not only by improving the classroom environment in general but by trying to alter it to ways that are most suited and preferred by a given group of students (Fraser 1986, pp. 165-66).

## Summary: Consistent Themes

We may draw a number of conclusions from the literature regarding the effect of school climate and culture on achievement. First, highly effective schools tend to emphasize teaching academic subjects, attaining subject matter competence, and acquiring basic skills; to have members who value academic excellence and expect high achievement and skill acquisition; and to have a staff that exhibits its high opinion of students' abilities. Such commonly shared attitudes may help lower students' sense of futility and increase their locus of control—important influences on individual achievement. Second, in effective schools, the building principal, or someone else, assumes the role of instructional leader. This person takes responsibility for students' achievement, develops and communicates plans for effective teaching, and nurtures cooperative relationships among all school members by being receptive and responsive to their needs. Third, effective educational environments maintain a pleasant and orderly atmosphere that promotes school coherence and positive, rather than competitive, relationships among the school's members. Fourth, in effective learning environments, students and teachers have positive feelings about their work setting. High morale appears to bolster the self-confidence of both teachers and students and promote positive attitudes and expectations about teaching and learning abilities.

The results from studies of effective classrooms closely parallel those from studies of school environments. In general, the attitude of teachers toward their students and their work coupled with the learning processes they establish shape the classroom's learning climate. In effective classrooms, teachers express high expectations for themselves and their students, positively reinforce their students' abilities and intelligence, spend quality learning time interacting with their students, and promote positive relationships among class members. Effective classrooms also have orderly environments that emphasize learning and academic activities, a commitment to learning, and the use of effective teaching strategies.

The importance of both noncognitive variables and effective management in the analysis of school and classroom climates is striking. The literature continually stresses the importance of both teaching and leadership skills and orderly, warm, supportive, and academically oriented environments. That is, academic achievement is enhanced when the normative structure of the group integrates high academic expectations with learning processes that emphasize interdependence, cooperation, and an orderly learning environment characterized by warmth, concern, and respect of others. Learning outcomes appear to be related to the ability of teachers and administrators to balance successfully the expressive or socioemotional and instrumental or task-related dimensions of both schools and classrooms. We return to this issue in Chapters 5 and 6.

# 3

# School Resources and School and Classroom Size

Chapters 1 and 2 examined how student groupings and the atmosphere or climate of a school affect learning. It is also possible that characteristics of schools more directly associated with the physical environment may influence achievement. In this chapter, we review literature describing how school expenditures and school and classroom size influence student achievement. In discussing expenditures, we cover the influence of per-pupil spending, facilities, and teacher qualifications on student achievement. In discussing size, we look at how classroom and school size affect student achievement and students' involvement in school. Although expenditures and size may appear to be variables quite apart from those discussed in the two preceding chapters, evidence suggests that they can be associated with students' behavior and attitudes and thus linked to their commitment to learning and achievement. In the last part of this chapter, we speculate on the nature of these connections as well as the difficulties involved in studying these areas.

Many studies have been completed in this area, most involving the so-called input-output approach. These studies generally use multivariate statistical techniques such as regression to assess the extent to which increasing "inputs," such as teachers' qualifications or per-pupil expenditures, affects "outputs," usually student achievement (Glasman and Biniaminov 1981). As in the other areas we have reviewed, results in this area are not uncontroversial, and it must be remembered that the final word is far from having been attained. Much of our review below depends upon meta-analyses and other large, systematic reviews of this literature. Such large-scale reviews, by assessing the extent to which results have been replicated and which studies use the best methodologies, are extremely important in supporting or disconfirming reported trends.

## School Expenditures

Section 402 of the Civil Rights Act of 1964 called for a survey "concerning the lack of availability of equal educational opportunities for individuals by reason of race, color, religion, or national origin in public educational institutions" (Coleman et al. 1966, p. iii). Underlying this mandate was the assumption that minority children had less access than white children to high-quality educational facilities and that these differential facilities contributed to their lower levels of achievement in school and in the adult world. This assumption has been a common one for many years; and, in fact, many studies, both before and since the one commissioned by Congress (Coleman et al. 1966), have examined the influence of a school's facilities and educational expenditures on students' achievement. In general, the results in this area of research are far from clear cut and far from as simple as those envisioned by members of Congress in 1964. Below, we discuss the results of studies that have examined how spending additional money on schools, either by enhancing facilities or as total expenditures, as well as the qualifications of teachers affect student achievement.

### SCHOOL FACILITIES AND PER-PUPIL EXPENDITURES

Despite common beliefs, most studies indicate that variables such as per-pupil expenditures and the presence or absence of school facilities such as libraries and science laboratories have little relation to students' achievement. Several extensive reviews of the literature and meta-analyses have reached this conclusion (Hanushek 1986, 1989; Bridge et al. 1979; Rossmiller 1982; Childs and Shakeshaft 1986). In general, only a minority of the studies show that greater financial support—including variables such as per-pupil expenditures, the quality of a physical plant, the age of a school building, the quality of a school's library, and the nature of school supplies—influences higher student achievement. These results appear in studies of both elementary and secondary students, with different measures of achievement (ranging from composite achievement scores and ability tests to achievement in various subareas), dropout rates, educational attainment, attitudes, and grades. They appear in samples from different regions of the country and with different levels of aggregation, that is, when the dependent variable is measured at the level of individuals, schools, or districts. They also appear when the studies reviewed are limited to those that use multivariate statistical techniques, which control for individual students' characteristics, and are methodologically strong in other ways (Hanushek 1986, 1989; Bridge et al. 1979).

Clearly, many studies indicate no relation or very small associations between greater expenditures and students' achievement. It is important to note, however, that, when a significant relationship does appear, it is usually in the expected direction, with higher average expenditures related (at least indirectly) to higher average student achievement (e.g., Bidwell and Kasarda 1975; Cohn and Millman 1975; Guthrie et al. 1971) and more elaborate and better maintained school facilities (e.g., Guthrie et al. 1971; Michelson 1970; Rutter et al. 1979; Phi Delta Kappa 1980) related to higher student achievement.

Joe Stone and Randall Eberts (personal communication) have noted that most of the studies included in these large-scale reviews do not match the resources available to the individual students who receive them. Instead, they generally look at the total resources available in a school and aggregate or individual-level measures of achievement. Using such aggregate measures assumes that all students in a school are the same and receive equal amounts of resources. This is clearly a questionable assumption. In fact, when studies do link individual students' achievement with the resources that they, as individuals, actually use, significant influences are much more likely to be found (e.g., Hedrick 1984). Similarly, the examination of specific budget areas, especially those with greater variability from one district or school to another, might be more likely to show significant effects. For instance, Fraser and associates (1986), using a large data set, note that the teaching budget directed toward science education significantly influences science achievement. Moreover, although few studies may show that the level of expenditures is related to student achievement, other studies indicate that the quality of a physical plant or environment is related to noncognitive outcomes, such as better attitudes toward school. These in turn eventually may be related to higher achievement (see Weinstein 1979; Mortimore et al. 1988, p. 222).

Despite the apparent simplicity of studying the impact of greater expenditures on student achievement, this is an area that is far from simple. In the last section of this chapter, we discuss a number of reasons why, despite the intuitive notion that strong associations should appear, they often do not.

## TEACHER QUALIFICATIONS

Teachers are clearly an integral part of the environment of schools, and schools and school districts have at least some control over the characteristics of teachers that they hire. As with facilities, this control can reflect the amount of money schools choose to invest in teachers. More money can be expended by simply paying teachers more than other districts or by hiring teachers who have more experience or years of education and thus earn more money than their less experienced and less educated counterparts. Many studies have examined how teachers' years of education; their years of teaching experience; the type of education that they have received, specifically the prestige of the school they have attended and their college major; and their own ability levels affect students' achievement.

As with the analyses of the influence of expenditures on educational outcomes, the results of the studies on teacher characteristics have been mixed. For example, Bridge and his associates (1979) reviewed a number of studies in this area, all similar to those involving school expenditures discussed immediately above and involving the "input-output" type of methodology. Only a minority of the studies reported significant influences of teachers' level of education on achievement; and half of these results showed a positive influence, while half showed a negative influence. Some studies, but again a minority of those reviewed, revealed that elementary teachers who had graduated from more prestigious schools had students with higher verbal or reading achievement. Slightly more than half of the studies showed that teachers with greater years of experience had students with higher achievement. Two thirds of the associations reported between teacher's verbal ability (most of which used the EEO survey data) were significant and positive, including the one that did not use the EEO data set (Hanushek 1972). More than half of the associations regarding teacher turnover were statistically significant, and a third of the studies involving the effect of teachers' salary were significant.

Other extensive reviews of the literature have found similar results or even fewer significant relationships, looking at teachers' years of education, teachers' experience, teachers' salaries, and quantitative measures of the quality of administrators (Hanushek 1971, 1986). The most impressive results found have been those involving teacher turnover, although the direction of causation in this area is certainly open to question. It is entirely conceivable, if not likely, that teachers would not want to leave schools or classrooms with high achievement patterns and that this causal pattern, rather than teacher longevity, can account for the strength of this relationship (see Finley 1984).

Bridge and his associates (1979) tend to place greatest emphasis on the effects of teacher training and teachers' verbal ability. Some studies indicate that teachers with more recent educational training or with more years of teaching experience have students with higher achievement test scores (e.g., Guthrie et al. 1971, p. 84). The effect of greater teaching experience, however, may be curvilinear, with the greatest effect in the first few years (Murnane 1975; Bridge et al. 1979, pp. 235-56). The other teacher-related variable with a relatively strong effect on student achievement is the teachers' own verbal ability. Studies, primarily those using the EEO study data (Coleman et al. 1966), have consistently shown a relationship between greater verbal ability of teachers and greater achievement of students (e.g., Armor 1972; also Bridge et al. 1979, pp. 249-51; Hanushek 1972).

Yet, as with the influence of expenditures, understanding the effect of teachers' characteristics on student achievement is far from a simple issue and may not be best tapped by the "input-output" studies reviewed in this section. From our discussion of the effects of classroom and school climate in the previous chapter, it is clear that schools and classrooms differ greatly in their effectiveness. Teachers and other school staff are central participants in the creation of these climates, yet the studies reviewed here have not captured these influences. In the last section of this chapter, we discuss some of the reasons for the lack of associations found here and speculate on more fruitful methods of inquiry.

## The Size of Learning Environments

Apart from the amount of money that is spent within schools, it is possible that the physical environment of schools—the surroundings in which students learn—can influence their achievement. Raymond Callahan (1962), in an extensive analysis of the historical development of today's departmentalized schools of several hundred, even thousands, of students, with classes of 30 or even larger, directly links these physical characteristics to financial constraints. He shows how these arrangements evolved in the early years of the twentieth century as school administrators tried to meet children's educational needs in the most economical and efficient way possible. (See Tyack 1974; Spring 1976; Cremin 1957; Katz 1968, for a variety of explanations of this historical era.) Since that time, there have been a great many studies on how the size of the classes and the schools children attend affect their learning. As with the analyses of financial expenditures and teacher characteristics, some interpretations of the results are not as straightforward as one might intuitively expect. The most extensive and complete analyses, however, suggest that students benefit most when they study in smaller classes and in smaller schools. We first discuss the literature on classroom size, then move to a discussion of the effect of school size, and then relate this material to our earlier discussions of effective learning climates.

## CLASSROOM SIZE

School officials may choose to spend available funds by hiring more teachers and thus reducing the average size of classrooms. As with school facilities and overall expenditures, the common-sense assumption is that students should do better in smaller classes than in larger classes, because more individualized attention should be associated with higher achievement.

Several large-scale reviews of literature in this area have noted very inconsistent results. The studies sometimes show that students have higher achievement in smaller classes, sometimes in larger classes, but most often the results are insignificant. Similar patterns seem to occur at all grade levels, with achievement test scores in a variety of areas, with ability test scores, and when either individual-level or aggregated data are used (Bridge et al. 1979; Hanushek 1986, 1989). Some suggest, however, that, when only studies with adequate controls and samples are examined, the vast majority favor small classes. Studies that have small samples and use inferior methodology are much more likely to show no effect or even to favor larger classes (Schieber et al. 1979).

Virtually all of these reviews focus on the results of regression equations obtained in the classical "input-output" studies of school effects. Such studies assume a linear relation between a dependent and independent variable and essentially indicate the extent to which increasing a class size by one student (or decreasing the teacher-student ratio by a given factor) alters a predicted level of student achievement. Such studies generally do not investigate the possibility of a curvilinear effect of class size on achievement. Nor do they examine the possibility of a "threshold effect," that is, that classes below a given number might be especially effective in increasing achievement.

A work published by Gene Glass and his associates in 1982 overcame these limitations by returning to the original studies and reanalyzing the entire body of results in a meta-analysis. After an extensive literature review, they found 77 studies, published between 1900 and 1979, that linked different class sizes to achievement. These involved 725 comparisons of larger and smaller classes. About half dealt with elementary classrooms and half with secondary classrooms. For their analysis, Glass and associates looked at the size of the small class, the size of the large class, and the average achievement scores of pupils in each class. They then standardized these mean differences and examined them within pairs of class sizes. In contrast to examining regression coefficients that summarize the changes in achievement as a linear trend, as in the studies reviewed immediately above, this allowed the comparison of achievement in one specific class size with achievement in another.

These comparisons led them to conclude that the greatest effects of class size appeared when very small classes were compared with larger classes, but that there were few differences when achievement in medium- and large-sized classes were compared. For instance, in comparing achievement scores of students in classes of 18 with those in rooms with 28 students, the achievement was greater in the smaller classroom in 69% of cases. When classes with 30 and 60 students were compared, those in the smaller classroom had higher average achievement scores only 50% of the time, the percentage that would be expected by chance. In contrast, in comparing classes sized 2 and 28, students in the smaller class had higher average achievement scores in 98% of the comparisons. Thus it appears that the effect of class size on achievement is curvilinear. Only when classrooms are smaller than about 15 students is it possible to see an increase in achievement. As classes fall below that size, the differential effect on achievement can be striking.

Not only do smaller classes affect achievement, they also appear to affect students' attitudes. Using a similar procedure to analyze studies of the effect of class size on outcomes such as pupil and teacher affect and instructional technique, Glass and his associates found odds of nearly 9 to 1 that smaller classes would have superior outcomes. They found that smaller classrooms more often had friendly environments, climates that were more conducive to learning, individualized instruction, more interested students, and less apathy, friction, and frustration. Teachers in smaller classes had higher morale, more time to plan their work, and greater satisfaction with their pupils and with their own performance (Glass et al. 1982, pp. 64-65).

In an attempt to expand upon these findings and determine more about how class size affects achievement, Cahen and associates (1983) developed an experimental case study in two elementary schools, one in rural Virginia and one in an urban, inner-city area of California. In these schools, they reduced the size of two classrooms by one third in the middle of the year by adding one teacher to each school. Data were gathered by extensive, naturalistic observation, field notes, interviews, systematic behavioral observations, and some achievement testing with the aim of understanding the naturally occurring changes that come with reduced classroom size. They noted changes in three broad areas: behavior management, individualization, and curriculum. Both the teachers and the more neutral observers noted that it was easier in the smaller classrooms to get students' attention and keep them engaged in learning activities. In addition, it was possible to have more individual contact time between students and teachers. This did not involve an individualizing of the curriculum, perhaps because of the short time in which smaller classes were used. Instead, there appeared to be a more effective, smoother, and often expanded and enriched coverage of the curriculum. The researchers suggested that this largely resulted from students giving more attention to learning and teachers giving greater attention to the needs of individual students.

## SCHOOL SIZE

Although many have intuitively assumed that smaller classrooms provide a better learning environment for students, much of the early literature suggests that larger schools and school districts enhance achievement. James Conant's influential book *The American High School Today* (1959) was especially important in prompting the development of larger high schools, no doubt far bigger than he envisioned at that time (Coleman et al. 1982, p. 164). He specifically denounced small high schools (pp. 77-85), believing that they were incapable of providing the curriculum thought necessary for the development of "comprehensive" high schools.

A paper distributed by the Wisconsin state superintendent of school's office (Fonstad 1973) illustrates how this view influenced policymakers. The report notes literature demonstrating that larger districts offer a broader range of courses and thus a more comprehensive educational program to students; more often have a complete range of educational services, either for remedial or gifted students; can more easily retain teachers, especially those with higher qualifications and specialized skills; and are more efficient than smaller districts, especially those with a small number of elementary schools. The common conclusion from this prescriptive literature is that students would be well served by the consolidation and reorganization of school districts to produce larger schools (see Dunne 1977; Rosenfeld and Sher 1977; Sher and Tompkins 1977, for reviews of the literature advocating school consolidation). Yet some research has tended to question these assumptions, focusing both on the effect of school size on achievement and on students' attachment to school.

*School size and student achievement.* A number of contemporary authors suggest that there is little direct or "net" association between the size of a school and students' achievement or other measures of educational "productivity." According to Sher and Tompkins (1977, p. 63):

> In recent years, researchers have begun controlling for IQ and social class. The effect of this development has been nothing less than a complete reversal of the traditional conclusions about the correlation between size and achievement. In fact, of the recent controlled studies, there is not one that records a consistent, positive correlation between size and achievement, independent of IQ and social class.

(See, e.g., Coleman et al. 1966; Aikins 1968; Raymond 1968; Krietlow 1962; all cited by Sher and Tompkins 1977.)

A number of studies also document a negative relationship between school size and student achievement once socioeconomic status and ability are controlled (e.g., Guthrie et al. 1971, pp. 86-90; Kiesling 1968; Summers and Wolfe 1977; Gregory and Smith 1987; Eberts et al. 1990; Mortimore et al. 1988). That is, students do better in smaller schools. The large EEO study (Coleman et al. 1966) found smaller school size associated with higher verbal achievement among 12th graders. In addition, there is little association between the size of high school a student attends and his or her grades in college (Downey 1978; Altman 1959).

The negative effect of school size may be greater for some students than others. For instance, further analysis of the EEO data indicates that the negative effect of size on achievement is stronger for black students than white students (Smith 1972, p. 291). Summers and Wolfe (1977) also note that smaller schools appear to benefit black students' academic achievement more than whites, and Willems (1967) notes that the negative effect of school size on involvement in school activities (see discussion of this general area below) is greater for marginal students.

*School size and student attitudes.* Simply noting that smaller schools may enhance student achievement does not indicate how this occurs. Literature that examines the effects of school size on other areas of student experience can provide clues to the nature of the process. In fact, this area is somewhat more developed (especially for high schools) than literature linking school size and achievement.

As noted above, those who have historically promoted school consolidation have suggested that larger schools enhance curriculum offerings, special services, and teacher quality. The empirical evidence supports these claims. Others suggest, however, that these earlier reviews ignored many of the advantages of small schools such as lower pupil-teacher ratios, more varied assignments for teachers, and better guidance and more attention available for individual students (Clements 1970; Dunne 1977; Gregory and Smith 1987). At least two studies (Bidwell and Kasarda 1975; Walberg and Fowler 1987) have found that smaller districts have higher average student achievement. Whether this effect occurs indirectly through the size of the pupil-teacher ratio (Bidwell and Kasarda 1975) or through the closer ties between parents, teachers, and administrators (Walberg and Fowler 1987; Coleman and Hoffer 1986), it suggests that the greater personal attention that occurs in smaller districts enhances achievement, at least on the aggregate level. Similarly, Lee and Bryk (1989) argue that, although school size has no direct effect on average school-level achievement, it strongly influences the amount of social and academic differentiation within schools—variables that are significantly related to student achievement.

Studies of elementary students suggest that small schools provide a more humanistic learning experience. They apparently do so by being able to more closely attend to the individual needs of each child (Day 1979), providing a more "open" environment (Flagg 1965), and being perceived by children as friendlier and more cohesive (Sinclair 1970; see also Kachel 1989). Studies of the relationship between social density (the number of students in a given space) and social behavior have been conducted with very young children in school-like settings and confirm these results. In general, they suggest that students in more crowded settings, which may occur more often in larger schools, are less attentive and less involved in activities (Weinstein 1979, p. 587).

Several studies suggest that students in small high schools are involved in a greater number and variety of activities, assume a greater number of positions of responsibility, are less alienated, and have a greater "sense of belonging" to the group than students in larger schools (Huling 1980; Barker and Gump 1964; Willems 1967; Baird 1969; Peshkin 1978; Turner and Thrasher 1970; Morgan and Alwin 1980; Wicker 1968, 1969; Downey 1978). These results occur in both urban and rural areas and particularly with students from lower socioeconomic backgrounds (Holland and Andre 1987). Because of their greater involvement, those in small schools report feeling needed and challenged, that they have an important job (Willems 1967; Wicker 1968). Many studies have linked these feelings of involvement with a lower probability of dropping out of school. Students who feel more identified with their schools are much more likely to remain in school until graduation (Finn 1989).

In addition, smaller schools have fewer discipline problems and less vandalism and crime (Duke and Perry 1978; Huber 1983). Coleman and associates' (1982, p. 164) analysis of the High School and Beyond data set notes that students in larger schools have slightly higher achievement once the incidence of behavior problems is controlled. In reality, however, the behavior problems are so much greater in larger schools that any possible virtue of larger size is canceled out by the difficulties of maintaining an orderly learning environment. Cusick's (1973) ethnographic study of a suburban high school vividly illustrates the alienation, fragmentation, and lack of involvement by most students that can appear in larger high schools.

Goodlad's (1984) extensive qualitative analysis of effective schools also notes that the schools that students and teachers find highly satisfying tend to be smaller than others. A sense of community is much stronger in small schools than in larger schools (Gregory and Smith 1987). Teachers in smaller schools are more satisfied with their work, have closer ties with each other and with their students, and feel more efficacious (Eberts et al. 1990; Gregory and Smith 1987; Newmann et al. 1989; Goodlad 1984; Mortimore et al. 1988). In general, smaller schools seem much more likely to exhibit the characteristics identified in our discussion of school climate as typical of the most effective schools. The schools are much more likely to be orderly and supportive; and both students and teachers have higher morale and a sense of connectedness and community. This can in turn prompt better relationships between administrators and teachers, and students may be more willing to accept and identify with an academic climate. (See Gregory and Smith 1987 for an extended discussion of the advantages of small schools and their climates.)

Barker and Gump, in their widely cited *Big School, Small School* (1964), provide one of the most developed explanations of these relationships. They suggest that, as schools increase in size, they increase in differentiation, but not at a continuous rate. Both large and small schools must fulfill similar functions, and, in fact, the smaller schools in their studies managed to sustain a larger proportion of activities than would be expected given their size relative to the larger schools. Thus students in small schools, in contrast to their counterparts in larger schools, must be involved in a wider variety of activities, both in participant and in leadership roles. This greater degree of responsibility can in turn help account for their lower levels of alienation and greater attachment to their schools as well as their better behavior (see Wentzel 1991).

The greater involvement of students in small schools does not extend across all activities, for, as noted by the literature promoting school consolidation, small schools often offer less variety in extracurricular activities than larger schools. Students in larger schools may actually have a greater chance to participate in hobby clubs, simply because these tend to be found only in larger schools. Most high schools have activities such as journalism, music, drama, athletics, and government; and students in smaller schools have a greater chance of participation in these areas than do students in larger schools (Morgan and Alwin 1980). Notably, it is these latter activities, more than individual hobbies, that would tend to bind students both to each other and to the school as an organization.

It is possible that the effect of school size on achievement may be related to the community in which schools are located and the ties of families and other community members to the schools (see Finn 1989, p. 130). For instance, a review of a number of studies using data from New York State found a negative effect of district size on student achievement but noted that the largest districts were also those in the most urban environments and that the degree of urbanness of a district, rather than size itself, might be the stronger influence on student performance (Irvine 1979, p. 54). On the other hand, the influence of involvement in school activities on students' attachment to school occurs in both large and small schools, and students in smaller schools are more likely to be highly involved. In addition, another study (Campbell, 1964) demonstrated differences in students' sense of "personal responsibility" among schools of different sizes, although they were all located in similar small rural communities, some of which (the larger ones) were consolidated and some of which were not. These results suggest that the effect of school size on students may well be independent of the effect of communities. We will, however, return to the issue of community effects in the next chapter.

## A Complicated Issue

Perhaps the most striking characteristic of the studies related to school expenditures is their general lack of strong relationships. Although the studies of school and classroom size yield somewhat more impressive results than those of per-pupil expenditures, school facilities, and teacher qualifications, none of the quantitative results could be described as strong. Some people, most notably Erik Hanushek, have taken this lack of striking results at face value, suggesting that it is difficult to relate the money that is spent on schooling to student outcomes and that policymakers ought to look to means other than greater school expenditures if they wish to enhance achievement (e.g., Hanushek 1986, 1989). Others have tended to focus on the few significant findings that do occur or dismiss the methods used in these studies as inappropriate and assert that school expenditures directly affect achievement (e.g., Guthrie et al. 1971; Spencer and Wiley 1981).

In contrast to these extreme positions, we suggest that, with the possible exception of using money to lower class size, there are few direct links between the allocation of funds within a school district and students' learning or achievement. It is probably unrealistic to expect strong relationships in this area for the relationship between expenditures and achievement is necessarily complex. The possibility of such associations should not be easily dismissed, however, and to determine the extent to which funds should be spent on schooling on the basis of simple correlations (or even regression equations) that describe the relationship between expenditures and achievement ignores the processes within school environments by which students learn. In this section, we discuss the complicated nature of the analyses reviewed above, first noting factors that may depress observed relationships and then discussing theoretical issues and results of other studies that help clarify the ways in which school expenditures affect student achievement.

## WHY THE REPORTED RELATIONSHIPS ARE SMALL

Intuitively, one would expect a positive relationship to appear between school expenditures and measures of student achievement. It is unrealistic to expect students to learn without adequate facilities, trained teachers, and suitable student-teacher ratios. The fact that studies indicate that associations in this area are often small or nonexistent leads researchers to look for possible explanations. The most common explanations involve the lack of variability in the measures, the possibility of nonlinear associations, and the practical problems of assigning funds to competing areas in schools and school districts.

*Variability.* It is important to remember that most of the work reported above has been done in the United States with data from public schools. Thus the studies have involved relatively little between-school variation in expenditures, facilities, class size, or even teacher qualifications. Districts do vary somewhat in the funds they allot to education. Yet all states have mechanisms to promote greater equity between districts both in expenditures, through various formulas of differential support, and/or in facilities, through requirements for certification. Federal and state aid to education also helps enhance school funding in the poorest of districts. Given these similar levels of financing, schools also differ relatively little in the average size of their classes. State laws about teacher certification tend to minimize differences in measurable qualifications of teachers, such as their training. Thus most studies of the impact of variables related to expenditures involve assessing the extent to which a little more or a little less of a given entity affects achievement. They cannot tap the effect of dramatic changes in the levels of expenditures. Certainly, if some community were to have *no* funding for their schools for a year, we would expect drastic differences in the achievement of students between communities. Such large variability, however, simply does not occur.

To compound the problem, some researchers artificially minimize variation. This can happen when aggregated measures of achievement and expenditures or other school or district characteristics are used. This procedure involves the implicit assumption that all students within a group receive equal benefits from the money allocated to a school or that they all have equal achievement levels.

A lack of variability in measures probably also accounts for many of the studies that report no association between school and classroom size and achievement. Input-output studies often have a sample of schools with only a small range of variation in school size (e.g., Rutter et al. 1979), a typical situation in a sample that only has schools in urban areas. Similarly, few districts have very small or very large classes, thus minimizing the possible comparisons. It is thus possible that even studies that indicate no relationship between achievement and school or classroom size have not provided an adequate test of the hypothesis. The meta-analytic techniques employed by Glass and his associates (1982) overcome this methodological limitation and report striking relationships between class size and achievement.

In addition to the presence of very little variation in facilities, expenditures, teacher qualifications, and school and classroom size, most of the studies in this area involve samples with a great deal of variability in students' socioeconomic and family backgrounds. It is logical to expect in these studies that more of the variation in student achievement could be explained by these individual-level characteristics than by the less variable school-level factors. In addition, the studies often involve very general dependent variables such as scores on norm-referenced achievement or ability tests. When there is greater variation among schools in facilities and expenditures, as can occur in other countries, the importance of school facilities and resources in accounting for achievement seems to increase. This appears to be especially apparent when the dependent variable involves subject exams that tap the curricular offerings in schools and when within-school student differences in family background are diminished (see Brimer et al. 1978; also Madaus et al. 1980). As we noted above, studies within the United States of specific content areas that are more likely to vary in support from one school or district to another, such as science, are more likely to show a relationship between funding and achievement (Fraser et al. 1986)

Certification requirements for teachers make it unlikely that studies in this area would include teachers with broad ranges of educational attainment. The results related to teachers' verbal ability, however, may illustrate how greater variability in teachers' characteristics may enhance the apparent utility of this measure. Even with relatively equal amounts of educational attainment, individuals can vary widely in their verbal skills. The fact that teachers' verbal skill is the one variable used in "input-output" studies for which moderately consistent influences on achievement have been found may at least partly reflect the fact that it is one of the few characteristics of teachers often used in these studies that has relatively more variation and thus the potential for demonstrating an effect.

*Nonlinear relationships.* Most studies in the "input-output" mode assume that there is a linear relationship between the independent and dependent variables. When the actual relationship is curvilinear, this assumption can result in an inaccurate report of no relationship. A curvilinear relationship can go unnoted with individual-level data simply because a researcher fails to look for it. When data are aggregated to the level of the classroom, school, or district, there is an even greater possibility of minimizing or ignoring a curvilinear relationship because the process of aggregation can mask the actual nature of the association.

The presence of a curvilinear relationship (as well as a lack of variability in the independent variables) no doubt accounts for the many studies of the effect of classroom size that reported no relationship. Smaller classes are more effective than larger classes only after a certain point (about 15 students). Once classes are larger than this, the effect of more students on achievement is much smaller.

It is also possible that the association between school size and achievement is not strictly linear. Very small schools and very large schools may both be detrimental to student achievement. Very small schools may provide too little stimulus and too few facilities for adequate learning; very large schools may be so alienating as to further suppress student achievement (see Coleman et al. 1966, p. 314; also Coleman et al. 1982, pp. 162-64). Support for the latter proposition comes from a study by Randall Eberts, Ellen Kehoe Schwartz, and Joe Stone (1990) of gain in mathematics achievement of children in elementary schools. They found only slight differences between achievement gain in small- and medium-sized schools once other relevant variables were controlled but a much larger negative effect on achievement when large- and medium-sized schools were compared. There appears to be a growing consensus that very large schools are detrimental to student achievement, and calls for division of such schools into "minischools" (e.g., Levin 1983) are becoming more common. Such changes may, however, have a beneficial effect only if the activity programs in the school are also displaced to provide greater opportunity for student participation (see Kleinert 1969).

*Trade-offs.* Closely related to the problems associated with the lack of variability of the indicators of school expenditures is the fact that schools almost always have a limited amount of funds to allocate. Thus it may well be fiscally impossible for a school district to maximize all of the possible areas of expenditure. If a district chooses to minimize class size, it may not be able to offer higher teacher salaries or have elaborate classroom facilities. Some evidence suggests that the ways in which schools allocate expenditures may be related to community types and community needs (Turner et al. 1986). It may indeed be possible that community types and student characteristics may interact in affecting the relationships between student achievement and school expenditures. We will return to this issue in the next chapter.

## UNDERLYING PROCESSES

Perhaps the most important reason the effect of school facilities and expenditures is small is that each of the variables generally measured when studying this area with an "input-output" approach is at least one step removed from the process of schooling itself (see Bidwell and Kasarda 1980). In other words, the various measures discussed in this chapter cannot tap the more subtle and complex processes that occur in schools and the ways in which individual teachers and students interact. This conclusion can apply both to the discussion of school expenditures and to the discussion of school and classroom size.

*School expenditures.* Measures of school expenditures typically look at the kinds of resources that are available, but not at how they are allocated. Simply looking at the amount of money spent in a school, the laboratory facilities, the years of education a teacher has had, or the number of students in a class does not indicate what actually happens within a classroom between students and teachers or between students. Knowing whether library books are actually read or the extent to which all students use science labs is probably much more important than simply knowing how many books are in a library or whether or not a school has a given number of laboratories (see Harnischfeger and Wiley 1980; Dreeben and Barr 1987; Barr and Dreeben 1983; Bidwell and Kasarda 1980; Brown and Saks 1980).

Similarly, simply looking at the number of years of education or experience a teacher has cannot tap the more subtle and lifelong influence of an outstanding teacher. Pedersen and associates (1978) have documented the effect of having a particular first-grade teacher on students' later lives. Even when various background characteristics were controlled, the long-lasting effect of having this effective first-grade teacher was direct and statistically significant. Numerous other studies have demonstrated that teachers vary greatly in their skills and effectiveness (Hanushek 1989; Brophy 1986; McLaughlin and Talbert 1990). Commonly used measures of teacher qualifications do not tap these differences, although more direct examinations of teacher behavior can do so (Hanushek 1989; Brophy 1986; Brophy and Good 1986).

One of the most important school resources related to achievement appears to be the time that students actually spend learning. Although the total amount of time that students spend in school varies relatively little from one school or classroom to another, the amount of time that students spend actively engaged in learning can vary a good deal more and is directly related to how much a student learns. How this active learning time is allocated in individual classrooms is a very important influence on achievement, but one that is not easily measured by the variables discussed earlier in this chapter. Studies that focus on the actual process of learning within classrooms, however, have consistently demonstrated that children's opportunity to learn the material is the most important link to achievement (Fisher and Berliner 1985; Brophy 1986; Brophy and Good 1986; Barr and Dreeben 1983; also see Carroll 1963 for a discussion of the theoretical underpinnings of this view).

More content appears to be covered in orderly, task-oriented classrooms where teachers hold high academic expectations and students are engaged in tasks that are not too difficult or too rote but that provide a high success rate. Jere Brophy emphasizes the importance of "active teaching," where teachers personally carry the content to their students rather than depending on curriculum materials to do the task and where they move through the curriculum "at an active pace" (Brophy 1986, pp. 1069-70; see also Brophy and Good 1986). As noted in our discussion of school climate, high achievement tends to be associated with teachers' warmth and responsiveness to students, their use of positive reinforcement strategies, their emphasis on cognitive development, and their good, but unobtrusive, control of their classrooms (e.g., Irvine 1979). It is not at all clear that any of these characteristics would be associated with the demographic variables commonly used in the "input-output" studies.

Teachers continually engage in decisions regarding the use of resources. Rebecca Barr and Robert Dreeben (1983, 1985) illustrate in their studies of elementary classrooms how teachers must continually make decisions regarding the allocation of resources within schools—involving the grouping of children, the time that will be devoted to teaching different groups, the allocation of curricular resources, and the pace at which children move through the material. None of these decisions is tapped by the typical input-output studies, but they each help determine how the resources within a school reach individual children. It is through these classroom and school-level decisions that resources affect achievement. (See also Bidwell and Kasarda 1980; Flinders 1989; Harnischfeger and Wiley 1980; McPartland and McDill 1982.)

The one teacher characteristic that tends to show consistent relations with student achievement is the verbal ability of teachers. We suspect that this relationship also reflects an underlying process and occurs because verbal ability, of all the teacher characteristics commonly measured in input-output studies, is most likely to be related to how teachers behave. It is entirely possible that teachers with greater verbal ability might be more likely to encourage higher-level cognitive development in their own students and challenge their students in ways that less verbally facile teachers could not. At the same time, unfortunately, teachers of higher socioeconomic background, who might be expected to have the highest verbal ability, tend to hold lower expectations for low-status and minority children (Alexander et al. 1987). This could increase pupil-teacher social distance, as well as teacher disaffection, and actually work against higher achievement.

Teaching is in many ways an art, requiring great sensitivity to the demands and needs of large numbers of students (Heck and Williams 1984). Jere Brophy, who has conducted extensive research on the actual work teachers do, contends that there can be no "teacher-proof curricula"; effective teaching depends upon the skills of individual teachers (Brophy 1986, p. 1071). At the same time, the literature also clearly suggests that some environments are much more conducive to effective teaching than others and that the conditions that enhance student achievement are also those that enhance effective teaching and higher teacher morale and satisfaction (Corcoran 1990; McLaughlin and Talbert 1990).

*School and classroom size.* Although the literature about school and classroom size has more significant results than that about facilities and teachers' qualifications, we again assert that it is the underlying classroom and school processes linked with size, rather than size itself, that are the important influences on achievement. As noted above, small classrooms tend to be distinguished by their greater behavioral control, more individualized instruction, and more enriched curriculum. Students in smaller schools tend to be characterized by their greater sense of personal efficacy, better self-concept, heightened sense of self-control, and better behavior. Significantly enough, literature on student achievement—from that of Coleman and associates with the EEO data (1966), to the more recent studies using the High School and Beyond data set, and school effectiveness and school climate literature—suggests that these variables have a strong relationship to students' achievement and to school effectiveness. In addition, some studies have suggested that greater opportunities for students to participate successfully in extracurricular school activities are related to a more positive school climate (Mitchell 1967; Epstein and McPartland 1976) and high student achievement (Rutter et al. 1979; Weber 1971; Hanks and Eckland 1976). In addition to greater involvement in school activities, it is possible that smaller schools can more easily develop consensus among members, both teachers and students, on curricular and disciplinary policies than large schools can. Students in smaller schools seem much more likely not just to behave better but also to believe that disciplinary procedures are fair (Coleman et al. 1982; Gregory and Smith 1987). Such consensus has been found to be related to more cohesive school climates (Wynne 1980), better student attendance, and higher academic achievement (McDill and Rigsby 1973; Rutter et al. 1979).

Most of the work on student involvement in schools has focused on secondary schools, probably because it is in these schools that extracurricular activities are more common. It is possible, then, that the causal linkages between school size and student achievement may involve different intervening variables depending upon the level of schooling that is studied. At the elementary level, the most important intervening variables may involve the humanistic atmosphere and individualized attention that are easier to attain in a small setting. At the secondary level, the most important intervening variables may be related to student involvement in the school and a sense of personal efficacy. On the other hand, these two variables may actually be elements of the same global phenomenon—a sense of belonging or meaning, or lower levels of alienation. They must simply be operationalized in different ways for children of different ages and in different types of schools.

Given the correlation between school size and students' sense of belonging or meaning, it could be expected that the various measures of school climate would be associated with the size of a school. It is surprising that there have been few direct tests of this hypothesis, although some studies provide preliminary evidence. For instance, McDill and his associates noted, in describing influences on various measures of school climate, that parental involvement in and commitment to the schools is the one contextual variable that is a source of climate effects (McDill et al. 1969; McDill and Rigsby 1973). Breckenridge (1976) notes that school climate can be improved by increasing communication and rapport between parents and school, while other studies (e.g., Phi Delta Kappa 1980 and see discussion in Chapter 4) suggest that greater parent-school and parent-principal rapport enhances student achievement. We would hypothesize that parental involvement would be related to both the size of a school and its relation to its surrounding community. We now turn to a discussion of community effects on achievement.

# 4

# Community Environments and Student Achievement

The previous chapters discussed the impact of school-related environmental variables on students' achievement. It is important to remember, however, that schools are embedded within communities—in neighborhoods, towns, and cities. Just as students may be influenced by their classmates, their teachers, and the norms and values within a school, they are influenced by the communities in which they live. Some of the influence of community environments on students is transmitted via the family, but some may also occur through the direct influence of communities on schools and often involves complex relationships among teachers, school administrators, students, parents, and other community members.

Communities vary a great deal in their economic, demographic, social, and political characteristics; yet, it is possible to outline ways in which community environments may affect achievement. In the first part of this chapter, we examine literature that describes the relationship of community environments to student achievement; in the second part, we discuss two issues that complicate theoretical generalizations in this area.

## How Communities Affect Student Achievement

Social scientists have long grappled with definitions of "community" and ways in which one may conceptually distinguish between various community "types." Traditional definitions have tended to focus on spatial or geographic characteristics, while more recent formulations have focused on community members, including their interactions, and their similarities and differences in ideologies and values. We recognize the complexity of developing a definition of community and that the issues involved in this area go far beyond those of concern to us here. Our major interest is understanding the relation of community environments, however they may be defined, to students' achievement and school success. In the sections below, we examine various aspects of this literature, each of which parallels, at least to some extent, the various definitions of community noted above. We include studies of neighborhood and community differences in achievement, the involvement of parents and other community members in the education of their children, and the influence of community differences in values on achievement.

### GEOGRAPHIC NEIGHBORHOODS

Traditionally, communities have been defined with spatial concepts. Classical distinctions have involved those between rural, urban, and suburban communities and between neighborhoods within cities, often defined by social status as well as geographic considerations (e.g., Rees 1970). Cities, suburbs, small towns, and even rural areas generally have a large degree of segregation related to social status variables and, when minority groups are present, to race and ethnicity as well.

It is not surprising then that studies reveal large differences between neighborhoods and communities in academic achievement, educational attainment, aspirations, and school climate measures (e.g., Turner 1964; Segal and Schwarm 1957; Rogoff 1961; Irvine 1979; Moos 1979; Trickett 1978). Although it is possible that such findings could result simply from an "ecological correlation," reflecting the high association between the social status of individual families and the communities in which they reside, many of the studies have introduced controls for the social status of the individual students. For instance, Rogoff (1961) examined the college plans and scholastic aptitude test scores of 35,000 seniors in 500 high schools, classifying the communities in which the schools were located into those in small towns, suburbs, and cities. After controlling for the socioeconomic status of the individual students and the differential dropout rates of the schools, she found the highest aspirations and test scores among students in the suburban schools. In a study involving high school boys in Los Angeles, Turner (1964) also found neighborhood differences in college plans, even when the students' socioeconomic status, ability group scores, and peer group pressures were held constant.

Similar results have been reported by a number of scholars (e.g., Sewell and Armer 1966; Garner and Raudenbush 1991). A recent study by Jonathon Crane (1991) documents the especially negative effects of living in the worst neighborhoods in large cities. Even after controlling for individual characteristics, such as family income, parents' educational status and occupation, household structure, and family size, he found that both black and white adolescents are more likely to drop out of high school when they live in the very worst neighborhoods. These "worst" neighborhoods do not differ incrementally from other slightly less deprived neighborhoods but are sharply different in the dropout rate and other problems exhibited by residents.

The most common explanation given in these studies for the apparent effect of community involves the notion of contextual variables and contextual influence, not unlike that noted for schools and classrooms in Chapter 1. It is suggested that, when lower-status students are surrounded by and thus have more contacts with higher-status students, they tend to increase their own aspirations (Krauss 1964). On the other hand, when they are surrounded by people with low aspirations and achievement, their own aspirations tend to suffer. As Boocock (1966, p. 39) puts it,

> A bright working class student's place of residence—or the school system's methods of assigning students to various schools—can determine whether he goes to a school which

> provides him with middle-class, college-oriented reference groups and reinforces any academic aspirations he may already have, or whether he goes to a school in which these same aspirations and abilities are neither recognized nor rewarded.

Just as the socioeconomic composition of a community influences the academic climate and expectations of a school, it also affects the resources that a school can offer its students. The resources available to a school district depend to a large extent on the nature of its industrial base and the socioeconomic status of its inhabitants. Although a school's facilities and resources reflect "a community's ability and willingness to finance education" (Day 1979, p. 32; see also Guthrie et al. 1971), the discussion in this chapter suggests that variations in total resources from one community to another, at least in the United States, are too small to affect achievement significantly. What appear to be more important are community decisions about the relative amounts of money that will be allocated to various resources, including teachers' salaries.

From analyses of the relation of resource allocations to the average achievement in school districts, Turner and associates conclude

> that school districts engage in policy maneuvers aimed at the marketplace of teacher talent and technical skills. These maneuvers derive from policy strategies aimed at reaching politically acceptable levels of student achievement while keeping per-student cost at politically defensible levels. These political constraints derive from the kind of community in which the school district operates. (Turner et al. 1986, p. 6)

From an analysis of empirical data from Colorado, they demonstrate that districts can enhance student achievement by devoting relatively more resources to financial rewards for teachers who obtain greater technical skills. The degree to which districts are free to do this depends on community-related variables including the size of the district (which allows certain economies of scale) and the wealth of the district.

As we note in Chapter 1, explanations of achievement that involve contextual effects, although supported by empirical evidence, do not tap the more subtle aspects of the processes involved in these influences. Similarly, examinations of the influence of communities that only use geographic or spatial definitions fail to tap the full complexity of the ways in which community-school relations may affect students. For instance, Steinitz and Solomon (1986) followed high-achieving working-class students from three different communities for four years after high school graduation. Their analysis demonstrates that communities and their schools affect not just the composition of individuals' reference groups but also students' self-conceptions and social identities. We turn now to more subtle and refined definitions of communities that go beyond the notion of group composition.

## COMMUNITIES AS INTERACTING GROUPS

The notion of communities as interactive units grew out of the desire to analyze community dynamics, to look at communities as more than ecological or spatial entities. Those who stress an interactive definition of community may retain the spatial notion discussed above but add to it the idea of communities as a "way of life, both . . . how people do things and what they want—their institutions, . . . collective goals, . . . [and] collective actions," the notion that "persons in a community should not only be able to, but frequently do act together in the common concerns of life" (Kaufman 1959, p. 9). They may emphasize the interactions between community members and the networks that result (e.g., Wellman 1979) and, at times, the importance of situational definitions of a community (e.g., Falk and Pinhey 1978).

The traditional notion of the neighborhood school suggests that interactions within a community may include, if not focus upon, the school. Yet historical patterns of changes in schools and school organization have tended to alter close community-school bonds. Below we examine historical changes in school-community relations and then turn to analyses of interactions between school officials and parents and community members.

*A historical perspective.* Much of the literature that examines the relationship between community environments and student achievement has focused on urban schools. Since the late nineteenth century, when waves of immigrants flooded cities in this country, educators and social reformers have tried to devise strategies to educate the cities' children. The major thrust of changes beginning in the late nineteenth century was the growing bureaucratization of schools, including the establishment of an age-graded curriculum and differentiation between the ranks of teachers and administrators. The end result of this process was the large and complex school systems found in cities throughout the country today. These systems often are so large that they allow little correspondence between schools and neighborhoods as interactive units. (See Tyack 1974; Spring 1976; Cremin 1957; Katz 1968, for a variety of explanations of this historical era.)

As schools in urban communities were trying to mitigate the alienation and powerlessness that appeared to be fostered by large, impersonal school systems, schools in rural communities had been drastically altered by the adoption of the urban model of school organization. School consolidation, the merger of smaller school districts into larger administrative units, swept the country. It was suggested that this consolidation would result in greater course offerings for students, more educational services, more efficient use of resources, and, by extension, higher student achievement (see Tyack 1974; Sher and Tompkins 1977; Rosenfeld and Sher 1977). The consolidation movement met with great success, and, during the twentieth century, the number of schools and school districts sharply decreased. From just 1950 to 1960, the number of school districts in the country was halved (Rosenfeld and Sher 1977, p. 39). In recent years, in the face of declining enrollments, many urban districts have also closed smaller schools to enhance efficiency and cut costs, with the same loss of community ties.

Studies suggest that the expectations associated with school consolidation have not necessarily been fulfilled. The shift to large-scale education has produced some economies, but school consolidation does not always lead to lower costs or greater efficiency. The economies that come with large-scale education tend to depend upon the density of the population in the area and the level of schooling involved (see Fox 1980; Sher and Tompkins 1977; Parks et al. 1982). In general, if students must be bussed a long way to school, the costs involved in transportation may well exceed the efficiencies gained in closing some schools.

In addition, consolidated schools are not necessarily of higher quality. A great deal of evidence notes that students in rural schools tend to have lower scores on standardized achievement tests and eventually attain lower levels of schooling. Residents of rural areas, however, are also more likely than those in other areas to lack proper medical care and to live in poverty-ridden conditions. Once differences in socioeconomic status and ability test scores are controlled, rural-urban differences in student achievement become statistically insignificant (see especially Sher and Tompkins 1977; also Kachel 1989, p. 94, and discussion in Chapter 3 regarding school size). Moreover, rural schools are more likely to have the elements of effective schools that were discussed in earlier chapters: smaller classes, greater student participation in extracurricular activities, orderly and safe environments, caring relationships between students and teachers, shared decision making and greater flexibility, and more community involvement and support (Jess 1989, pp. 43-44, cited by Pepple et al. 1990).

Ironically, one reason often cited for the lack of improved quality in consolidated schools is the diminished ties between the community and the school that result when students must travel far from their homes to attend classes (see Campbell 1964). Attempts to consolidate and close schools can often meet with intense opposition from affected communities and families as they realize the extent to which the school-community ties will be altered. (See Peshkin 1982 for a description of a particularly protracted controversy over school consolidation and closure.)

A number of school reform attempts can be seen as attempts to reestablish these community-school ties and can be understood by using the notion of communities as interactive groups. Examples of these reforms include parental involvement in education, community education, and community control of schools. Although each of these involves attempts to improve the relationship between parents (and sometimes other community members) and schools, they reflect different amounts of relative control or influence of community members on the schooling process, from those in which the school retains its traditional power to those that involve explicit attempts by community members to have more voice in the schooling of their children.

*Parental and community involvement in schools.* One way to involve community members in schools is as adjuncts to the educational process, serving as aides in the classroom, helping students with homework, or helping school employees complete their tasks in other ways. Parental participation in schools is generally described as a way for parents to learn more about what their students are doing in school and as a way to improve children's behavior and interest in school. Teachers may encourage parents to participate in a variety of ways, from listening to their children read or discussing assignments with their children, to informal home learning activities, formal agreements or contracts between the teacher and parents to assist the students, even to training parents in effective teaching methods (Moles 1982; Cervone and O'Leary 1982; Gonder 1981; Bauch 1990).

A large amount of evidence now supports the view that parental involvement is an important ingredient in improving individual children's achievement and in enhancing school effectiveness. Involvement as minimal as simply attending school events and meetings seems to help enhance achievement. Both large, nationally representative studies and smaller studies of only a few schools indicate that students whose parents are actively involved in the school—by participating in classrooms and school meetings or attending school events—tend to have higher achievement and better attendance, behavior, and grades, as well as higher self-confidence, regardless of their ethnicity or social class (Henderson 1988; Stevenson and Baker 1987; Bauch 1988; Dornbusch and Ritter 1988; Mortimore et al. 1988; Collins et al. 1982). Parents' active involvement in schools also affects the motivations of both teachers and students, raising their expectations for academic achievement. Moreover, parental activism has successfully influenced government funding.

Evidence also suggests that strong bonds between schools and the surrounding community help enhance school effectiveness

(Fullan 1990; Henderson 1988; Silver 1990; Koziol 1990). Local businesses may help schools through various career education and work experience programs. The use of community resources in classrooms is described as a way to "extend curriculum and at the same time relieve strain on teachers" (Miranda 1983). It also helps establish and maintain interactions between school officials and community members and to increase the public confidence in the schools. Rumors within a community regarding school activities can often exacerbate school-community tension, especially when schools are trying to desegregate or institute other changes (e.g., Schofield 1982). When close ties are developed and maintained between school and community officials, these rumors can be more easily discounted, and desegregation efforts and other moves toward more effective schooling can be more successful (Raffel 1980).

It is important to note that this parental and community involvement almost always occurs in a context that is defined and controlled by school officials (Lightfoot 1978; Bastian et al. 1986). In fact, it has been suggested that such community involvement is only successful when it is initiated, or at least welcomed by, school teachers and administrators (Gonder 1981, Weinberg 1983). Greater involvement of parents, especially in working-class and minority communities, seems to be enhanced when teachers have more positive and understanding attitudes toward parents and develop an ability to communicate and work with parents in an open, collaborative manner, an issue we return to later in this chapter (Bauch 1988; Henderson 1988; Lightfoot 1978; Epstein 1988; Leitch and Tangri 1988; Power and Bartholomew 1987; Lareau 1989; Comer 1991).

*Community education.* Beyond simply involving parents and other community members in the regular education program, schools may expand their educational focus to encompass the entire community. The Community Education movement explicitly tries to do this through "community schools." This movement defines *education* broadly, to encompass all the various resources of a community that help individuals cope with their environment. Community schools are seen as one way of accomplishing this goal by being a focal point for cultural, recreational, and educational activities. The schools were first proposed as a way to combat not only educational disadvantage but also delinquency, poverty, and general urban decay (see Olsen 1953; Fantini 1970).

School districts that try to develop community schools accept several general responsibilities: developing an educational program for school-age children; making school facilities as available as possible to community members; providing additional after-school programs for children, youth, and adults; serving as a distribution point for community services; and helping to develop community councils that allow community members to identify and solve common problems. Community schools are usually based in elementary schools in an explicit attempt to use the attendance area for the school as a community or neighborhood base. The principal of the school is accountable for the various components of the community school, and various staff members and volunteers coordinate programs such as recreational services, adult education programs, and health services (Minzey 1981; McCloskey and Harrison 1983; Baas 1973).

The Community Education movement expanded greatly during the 1970s, in large part due to the support of the Mott foundation. Like the attempts to involve parents and community members in schools, this movement helps to increase interactions between school personnel and community members. It goes beyond simply helping to maintain the ongoing school processes, however, and attempts to expand school services outside the traditional school boundaries and to encourage "participatory democracy" or community involvement in neighborhood problem solving.

Yet community education is school based. Although it may encourage community members to work together to solve neighborhood problems, it does not challenge the basic structure of authority in the schools. Responsibility for implementing and maintaining community education is largely in the hands of school officials. Community-controlled schools try to alter this.

*Community-controlled schools.* A counterpart of the growing complexity of school systems is a decline in the control that local communities have over schools in their neighborhoods. Traditionally, schools have been the one area of government, other than cities, over which individual citizens have had the greatest control and access to policy decisions. They can elect representatives to school boards, can actively voice their complaints regarding their schools to these board members, and can have a fair amount of influence on the tenure of district superintendents (Callahan 1962; Lutz 1990). As school districts have become larger, either with the growth of cities or through consolidation of smaller districts, the ability of individual citizens to directly influence their neighborhood schools has declined.

In an attempt to counter this process, various reformers in the 1960s promulgated the idea of "community-controlled schools" (see Fantini et al. 1970). The aim of these schools was not just decentralization of the bureaucratic apparatus of large school systems but direct involvement and control by community people over the functions of neighborhood schools. The movement received the most popular attention in urban, minority neighborhoods. Unlike parental involvement and community education, community control aims at allowing the school to reflect the values and culture of the community it serves and giving the community the power necessary to improve its children's education. Proponents advocated community control as a way of strengthening the power of minority neighborhoods, reducing racial tension, and improving the quality of education for urban minority children (Davis 1970; Bourgeois 1969; Cohen 1969; Barraclough 1973).

The most extensive experiments with community-controlled schools in urban areas occurred in the late 1960s in New York City. With the financial support of the Ford Foundation, three experimental decentralized districts were established in African American communities. Because of political crosscurrents and especially the opposition of the teachers' union, however, the experiments met with little success. A school decentralization law passed in 1969 allowed for the election of local, neighborhood school boards but left the control of personnel and money in the hands of the central school board. These restrictions meant that the local boards had no effective control over the schools in their area.

In a recent analysis of urban school reform, Michael Williams (1989) suggests that community control of schools is not as effective a mechanism of school reform as the participation of community members in school governance along with other responsible parties. In this analysis, he advocates the approach of Bruce Joyce, Richard Hersh, and Michael McKibben (1983), who have called for a collaborative model of school governance. In this model, representatives from the general public, administrators, teachers, technical consultants, and parents and students would all have an effective voice in school governance. Williams argues that it is unrealistic for communities to believe that they can "control" a school but they can realistically work with other responsible groups to help develop effective schools that are, as he puts it, "in control" (Williams 1989, p. 69). He further suggests that the most realistic political tool for helping to attain this voice in school governance is neighborhood organizations and suggests that parents and others interested in neighborhood school reform should work with existing multiple-issue and politically experienced neighborhood organizations (see also Comer 1980; Chavkin 1990).

Community control of schools has never been fully implemented in a large city system. Although the term *community control* has generally been avoided in recent years because of the failures in New York City, decentralization of school authority with greater neighborhood control of local schools has been proposed for and attempted in a number of large cities. The potential for any extensive parental control over neighborhood schools in these settings appears to be small, however, given the intransigence of large bureaucratic school systems and the distrust that often appears between parents and school officials (see Seeley and Schwartz 1981; Davies 1981, and the discussion below). Perhaps, however, as we discuss more thoroughly in Chapter 6, it is realistic to expect that parents and other community members could have more influence on school activities if school officials were to realize the benefits of such policies.

One of the most difficult political aspects of advocating community control in large urban areas is that, given the extensive racial segregation of urban neighborhoods, community control usually works directly against the aim of racial integration. Because communities are often racially segregated, so are community- or neighborhood-based schools. Early advocates of community control in New York City suggested that giving minority group members a greater voice in their children's education would help mitigate racism embedded in the school system. Although many liberal civil rights advocates were supportive of the movement, many were also uncomfortable with it, believing that it reinforced segregation. More contemporary calls for community control, often described as "neighborhood schools," have often been only thinly disguised pleas for segregation, supported by white, antibussing advocates (see Seeley and Schwartz 1981).

As noted above, an important influence on students' achievement is the composition of a classroom and school. The aim of most desegregation efforts is to alter the composition of schools and classrooms to develop a mixture of students of various backgrounds. Community control, by emphasizing the neighborhood context of schools, can work directly against this aim. The extent to which community control, by giving minority parents a voice in their children's education, can mitigate the problems of segregation is not clear.

## COMMUNITY VALUES AND STUDENT ACHIEVEMENT

In the sections above, we have defined *community* as a spatial entity, using the notion of neighborhoods and noting the importance of interactions of community members. Beyond this concept of interactive groups within spatial boundaries, it can be suggested that members of communities develop shared values from their social relations (Christenson 1984). Obviously, not all people who live in contiguous areas or who interact regularly come to share common values. Thus this notion of community, as people who interact with each other and share common values, is the most restrictive we have used.

Perhaps because it is extremely difficult for community members and parents to develop a voice in the governance of their public schools, enrollment of students in nonpublic schools rose quickly in the 1970s and 1980s. Because people choose to be affiliated with a private school, it is reasonable to assume that private school constituents are more homogeneous in their attitudes toward education and values than are those in comparable public schools. Moreover, because private schools can exist only with the support of parents and students, it is also possible that parents would have more influence over the governance of a private school than over a public school.

Using the High School and Beyond data set, which includes students from more than 1,000 public and private high schools, James Coleman and his associates (1982; Coleman and Hoffer 1987) conclude that those who attend private and parochial schools have consistently higher achievement and educational aspirations, more often attend college, and less often drop out of high school than their peers in public schools, even after controlling for individual variables such as socioeconomic status. Minority students from more deprived backgrounds tend to benefit the most from attending private schools (Greeley 1982; Coleman and Hoffer 1987; Hoffer et al. 1987). These achievement differences do not reflect variations in individual characteristics of the students or the financial resources of the schools as much as variables more closely related to school climate. Students in private and parochial schools tend to behave better, to be more committed to academic values, and to have better attitudes toward their schools. Coleman and his associates contend that it is these climate and attitudinal differences that can account for the variations in achievement between public and private schools. In fact, public schools with climates like private schools have equally high achievement levels. They suggest that most of the differences between private and public schools can be attributed to the consensus within the community affiliated with the private and parochial schools regarding academic values and achievement.

Coleman (1987c, p. 197) uses the term *value community* to describe "a collection of people who share similar values about education and child rearing." Although he notes that principals in public schools with "strong personal force" can sometimes create such a community within a school, it is always open to challenge from parents, students, or others within or outside the school. Within private and parochial schools, however, such a value community can occur quite naturally as parents and students voluntarily choose to enroll their children in a school and, in fact, pay for the privilege of doing so. Presumably, because they have chosen to enroll their children in the school, they share the values espoused by the school staff and other parents and thus help to support the value community. Coleman suggests that such schools are much easier to teach in and to manage. The greater orderliness of the school and the commitment of teachers, parents, and students to the school help make it more effective.

A smaller, qualitative study by Douglas Kachel of parochial schools in the Amish community confirms these results (Kachel 1989). Typically, in these rural, one-room schools, about 30 students from age 6 to 14 are taught by an Amish teacher, who generally has no high school education. There are no special programs and the facilities would be considered crude by modern, urban standards, often with no indoor plumbing or electricity. Yet the students consistently score as well as or better than national norms on standardized tests of achievement in all areas but vocabulary, an understandable result given the fact that, for most of the children, English is a second language.

Kachel's description of the schools and their community suggests that these results reflect the association between the Amish schools and the community and the values that they mutually support. All children are expected to do well in school, and "cooperation, group harmony, mutual respect, and the need for interdependence are encouraged and approved" (Kachel 1989, p. 95). There are no social class distinctions in the community or school; all children dress alike, and there is "a strong sense of equality and mutual acceptance" (1989, p. 95). The teacher-student relationship is warm and personal, and parents and community members are highly involved in the operation of the school. Kachel suggests that these characteristics allow Amish children to grow up without the negative experiences that can be associated with continual competition and the lack of achievement so common in public schools. Because the Amish family is highly stable, with a very low divorce rate, Amish children experience consistent nurturance and support in both their homes and their schools. As Kachel (1989, p. 97) notes, "from this strong, supporting, social network of family and school, the Amish child continues to develop his or her feelings of positive self-worth and confidence in addition to a growing sense of commitment to community values and responsibilities."

These strong value communities no doubt help enhance what James Coleman calls "social capital." Social capital is not as much a characteristic of individual people as it is a resource for individuals. It comes from the relationships that people have with others, for, according to Coleman, social capital "exists in the *relations* among persons" (1988, pp. S100-S101, emphasis in original). It involves obligations, behavioral expectations, and trust that develop from strong ties among individuals in a group; channels of information that help people be more informed; and norms and effective sanctions that both facilitate and constrain certain actions. Although family relations are one source of social capital, relations with others in a community also enhance it. Children who have strong, dependable, and extensive relations with other people—both inside and outside the family—have more social capital. Both Coleman's (1988; Coleman and Hoffer 1987) and Kachel's (1989) works indicate that social capital is an important influence on educational achievement and attainment.

## CONCLUSION: COMMUNITIES AND ACADEMIC ACHIEVEMENT

The literature reviewed above implies that students' achievement would be enhanced if they attended school in a community with a large number of high-achieving peers, whose members are able to interact with each other and with school officials, where community members and parents can be involved with the school, and, finally, and perhaps most important, if in these interactions mutual respect and common values that support achievement could be developed.

The community education and community control movements have different political and theoretical suppositions. Yet they both have the aim of tying community members more closely to school operations and the implicit assumption that such ties would enhance student achievement and the effectiveness of the cities' schools. As we noted above, evidence indicates that good relationships between schools and parents and between communities and schools can enhance academic achievement, school climate, and school effectiveness (Breckenridge 1976; Phi Delta Kappa 1980; Henderson 1988; Stevenson and Baker 1987; Bauch 1988; Dornbusch and Ritter 1988; Mortimore et al. 1988; Collins et al. 1982).

It is possible to further examine the relationship between the various concepts of community discussed in this chapter. Some geographic settings may make parental involvement and identification with the school easier. Observers of schools in rural settings have noted the identification of students and parents with their schools. In these settings, not just parents and students but the entire community often tend to be strongly identified and involved with school-related activities (Dodendorf 1983; Kachel 1989; Schmuck and Schmuck 1990; Pepple et al. 1990; Eberle 1983; Peshkin 1978). Similarly, a broad study of a large number of rural Alaskan schools (McBeath et al. 1983) notes that schools with "localized control" have the lowest rates of absenteeism and vandalism of all the schools studied, perhaps indicating a greater degree of identification with the school itself (see also Dunne 1977). If one accepts the findings noted above regarding the relationship between parental involvement with the school and school climate and student achievement, these results would suggest that schools in a community setting that promotes strong identification and ties of parents and students with the school might be more likely to foster more effective school climates, once variables such as socioeconomic status of the parents are controlled. This more effective school climate may in turn be related to greater student achievement.

It is important to avoid romanticizing rural communities, for it is clear that the isolation and typically lower average educational attainment of people in these communities often work against the possibility of educational advantages (see Dunne 1977; Sher and Tompkins 1977; Pepple et al. 1990). A close fit between a school and its community is also not without problems. Peshkin (1978), in a study of a rural community and its high school, notes the dilemmas that arise from this close fit. Although the close-knit community results in feelings of belonging, commitment, and social support, it also promotes insularity, a retention of values and perspectives associated with this insularity, and a limited emphasis on academic achievement. It can also promote unique problems for teachers, especially those who perceive themselves to be different from powerful people in the community (McPherson 1972).

In commenting on this situation, Hamilton (1983) notes the limitations in students' outlooks that such close ties may promote, but suggests that the personal and societal value associated with these ties, including self-confidence and commitment, should not be lightly dismissed, especially given the relatively small differences in the academic achievement of students in rural, small schools compared with that of students in the nation as a whole. Such ties probably reflect what James Coleman has called a "functional community," a community in which people are much more likely to know and interact with parents of children's friends. In such communities, parents are more aware of what is happening to a child and at the school, and adults are more likely to take an interest in other people's children. As we noted above, this produces social capital, an important resource in promoting children's achievement and well-being. Although Coleman notes that such communities, through "exclusionary and separatist tendencies," can produce parochial and insulated orientations toward the world, they also provide extensive support networks for both parents and children. In addition, they can promote value communities, which, as we note above, can be an important ingredient in effective schools (see Coleman 1987c, pp. 182-97). The challenge for those concerned with quality education may well lie in promoting strong ties between communities and schools, supportive interpersonal environments, and an academic climate that encourages each participant to achieve to his or her potential, no matter where a school is located.

## Complicating Factors

As with the other topics that we have discussed, understanding community influences on educational outcomes is not simple. In this section, we discuss only two issues that contribute to this complexity: variability among and within communities and political power and conflict.

### VARIABILITY

In any discussion of communities, it is important to remember that they differ a great deal. The most obvious differentiating factor is size; some are larger than others. They also vary in contiguity to metropolitan areas, as in the classical distinction of urban, rural, and suburban areas, and in their available cultural and recreational opportunities. Communities vary a great deal in income and in their industrial or economic base, with some being much wealthier than others and with greater occupational opportunities. Similarly, communities may have different dominant values. Some may be much more likely than others to espouse the importance of educational achievement and educational equality. Communities may also differ in their age distribution and specifically in their proportion of young people. Finally, communities may vary in their stability: the extent to which their population composition and economic characteristics have changed over the years.

In addition to this variation among communities, there may be a great deal of variation within a community. There is often racial-ethnic diversity as well as diversity in educational attainment, income, political power, and values. Some communities are more heterogeneous than others, with greater diversity in residents' demographic backgrounds, greater variation in economic resources, and greater diversity in values and orientation toward education.

Both the type of community and the amount of variation within a community can influence the achievement of children in schools. Diversity among communities certainly affects resources that a school can provide and the status composition of a school. The work of Turner and associates (1986) demonstrates how different types of communities may need to allocate resources in different ways to enhance achievement. Small districts and schools may use lower pupil-teacher ratios (smaller classes), often by default because they have so few students. Larger districts and schools, which can take advantage of the economies of size, may elect to increase class size and invest the saved resources in incentives for teachers to increase their skills and training. Communities with larger populations of low-income and bilingual or poor minority students may need to invest additional resources to address their specific needs. The demographic makeup of a community, its economic circumstances, and its political orientations can also affect the relationships between school districts and teacher unions as well as the stances taken by unions (Jessup 1985). These variables, as well as the size of a school district, can also affect the nature of political relationships surrounding school-related issues (see Eaton 1990).

Within-community differences are much more likely to affect the interactions that occur in a community surrounding a school. For instance, communities with larger proportions of residents without school-age children may face greater political resistance to attempts to enhance school effectiveness. Communities with more variation among residents in income, educational attainment, and racial-ethnic background may have more variation in education-related values and certainly more diversity in the power and influence of community members in the schools. The amount of within-community variation is no doubt related to the way conflict appears in schools and school districts and the way it evolves and affects students.

## COMMUNITY CONFLICT

A variety of actors are present in any school situation: students, parents, other community members, teachers, administrators, and other school staff. Each of these groups, to one extent or another, may be concerned with issues involving the schools and have different political agendas, different motivations, and different power bases. The nature of these differences may vary from one community to another, but it is important for any analysis of the influence of communities on schools to understand the different agendas, interests, and values of the actors in the situation and how these differences affect students.

Social scientists approach conflict in a variety of ways, some emphasizing its presence in many aspects of life and others diminishing its importance. It is no doubt true that only a minority of community-school interactions actually involve overt conflict, yet it is clear that parents and community members may often have concerns about and goals for schools that differ from those of teachers and administrators. For instance, parents are much more concerned with what Talcott Parsons has called particularistic expectations regarding their own child, although teachers and other school officials are more concerned with universalistic expectations (Parsons 1959; see also Dreeben 1968). Parsons, as well as Willard Waller (1932), emphasizes that these different orientations of families and schools are functional, or useful, for the society, in that families help provide a nurturant, loving basis for the growth of the child's self-esteem, while schools help to introduce the child to the larger society and the achievement-oriented goals and orientations found outside the family.

To some extent then, uncomfortable relationships, even hostilities, between parents and teachers are to be expected given the teachers' different orientations toward students and their different role assignments (see especially McPherson 1972); and, moreover, they may well be functional as they help children separate from the insular world of the family. Yet, as Sarah Lightfoot (1978, p. 41) has noted,

> These discontinuities between families and schools become dysfunctional when they reflect differences in power and status in this society. When we perceive the origins of conflict as being rooted in inequality, ethnocentrism, or racism, then the message being transmitted to the excluded and powerless group (both parents and children) is denigrating and abusing. When schooling serves to accentuate and reinforce the inequalities in society, then it is not providing a viable and productive alternative for children.

The extent to which the inherent differences between parents and community members on the one hand and teachers and other school officials on the other become dysfunctional thus no doubt varies from one community to another. The extent of this variation depends upon the demographic characteristics of the communities, their heterogeneity, the makeup of the school staff, and the history of school and community relations, but it also probably depends upon the possibility that parents and community members can effectively voice their differing concerns. This may well depend upon the extent to which schools have managed to implement and maintain some mode of a collaborative governance structure such as that proposed by Bruce Joyce and his associates (1983).

Although it may not be overt, the potential of community-school conflicts and questions of who will decide what issues and in what way are probably always present. Mary Metz (1990) has described how differences in the social class composition of communities influence the nature of the school-community link. Although students in different types of communities clearly differ in their skills, more important differences appear in their attitudes toward studying and the importance of school subjects as well as in the influence that the parents and community members have over the school. Both parents and students are more involved in their schools in higher-status communities, but, even more important, given their high status, parents and community members in higher-status areas have much more power and control, both individually and collectively in their interactions with the school. Partly because the lower-status communities in Metz's study were in large cities with heavily bureaucratized school systems, but also because the parents were of lower status than the teachers and because they were less skilled in negotiating and dealing with bureaucracies, parents in these lower-status communities had much less influence on their schools. (See also McPherson 1972, and Lareau 1989, for extensive discussions of how teacher-parent differences in social status affect interactions.)

In her description of parent-teacher conflicts over school-related issues in large, urban districts, Sarah Lightfoot notes that these conflicts may be a necessary and inevitable by-product of the different environments and goals of families and schools. Yet she also suggests that greater communication and interaction between families and schools, "learning about each other's values, styles, and modes of communication" (Lightfoot 1978, p. 189), is a necessary part of enhancing students' schooling experiences and can help counteract the alienation and dysfunctional aspects of many parent-teacher interactions. She suggests that conflict can be productive and help produce better understanding by parents and teachers of each other, but that this "productive conflict must arise out of some level of harmony and unspoken consonance (which must be consciously developed and deliberately nurtured if families and schools are culturally divergent)" (Lightfoot 1978, p. 189).

Laurie Leitch and Sandra Tangri (1988) reach similar conclusions based on their observations of the relationship between parents and teachers in low-income, largely African American schools in Washington, DC. They note the significant barriers to effective home-school collaboration in this situation but assert that sensitive planning and coordination, with continual reevaluation of the success of the efforts, could lead to more productive relationships (see also Comer 1991).

Although teacher-parent conflicts may focus more on the experience of individual students, those that pit parents and community members against school administrators may more often involve general school policies. Ostensibly, schools in the United States are controlled by communities through locally elected school boards. (Notably, this local control is much greater here than in most industrialized countries.) Citizens not only elect the boards but may bring issues of concern to the boards and participate in regular meetings. In communities throughout the country, school boards and communities may become embroiled in intense issues ranging from curriculum to discipline to staffing to issues surrounding desegregation. (See Schofield 1982, and Raffel 1980, for discussions of community concerns regarding desegregation of schools.) School policies are approved by the elected boards, yet professional administrators are hired by the boards to implement these policies. (See Wirt and Kirst 1982 for an extensive discussion of these relations.)

Given this official notion of community or lay control through locally elected school boards, it is important to ask what actually happens when policy decisions are made. Harmon Zeigler and his associates have extensively studied actual decisions made by school boards and the participation of school board members, school superintendents, other administrators and school professionals, the public, and other government units in these decisions (Zeigler and Jennings 1974; Zeigler and Tucker 1981; Tucker and Zeigler 1980). They conclude that the role of the superintendent and other school professionals is central in these decisions. The development of proposals to be presented to the school board is clearly dominated by superintendents, and school boards generally expect and honor recommendations for action by superintendents. The evidence suggests that school boards look to their hired staff as experts in the field of education and, more often than not, defer to their opinions in making policy decisions.

Even within small rural communities, with an extensive “family spirit” surrounding the schools, formal collegial collaboration in governance appears to occur very rarely (Schmuck and Schmuck 1990). Community control through school boards is thus at most a filtered process, with much of the decision making greatly influenced by professional educators.

## Summary

Community environments may affect students in a variety of ways. Simply as the context in which schools are located, communities affect the composition of a student body and the nature of school support and facilities. Yet communities are more than spatial entities, and the relationships between schools, families, and communities also affect students. Over the years, school consolidations and closures have clearly affected the school-community bond, and educators in recent years have tried to reestablish these ties. Attempts to involve parents in their children's education provide an important boost to children's achievement, but it appears important to have this involvement occur within a supportive and collaborative relationship that values and respects the input of parents. Attempts to develop community schools and to have community-controlled schools have explicitly tried to develop more extensive ties between parents and community members and the schools. Community-controlled schools, in particular, have tried to alter the balance of power between parents and schools, although they have met with little success.

Communities may also be defined as groups that develop shared values. Recent research has demonstrated the extent to which the values inherent in a school's community help enhance students' achievement. Students in schools, both public and private, that involve communities that advocate and support strong academic values tend to have higher achievement. Communities that value academic achievement and also can provide interpersonal support or "social capital" to students tend to have schools where students have the highest levels of achievement.

In the last sections of the chapter, we discussed how variations from one community to another and conflicts within communities can affect these generalizations and relationships.

The issues of variability and conflict are only two of the complicating issues involved when discussing the relationship between communities and student achievement. In the next chapters, we return to these issues and others as we describe theories that can help explain the relation of educational environments to student achievement. We then discuss the implications of these notions for public policy and for future research.

# 5

# Individuals and Their Environments: Theoretical Views

In the last four chapters, we reviewed a large body of literature regarding the effects of environments on students' achievement. Although it must be remembered that new research in these areas will continue to appear, a number of conclusions seem reasonable based on the current state of the literature. For instance, our discussion of the groupings in which students learn suggests that, with only a few exceptions, more heterogeneous groups promote student learning. Minority students do better in desegregated schools, especially when they enter these settings in the earliest grades. Students also tend to show higher achievement in settings with more high-ability and high-status students and when they are not tracked into lower curricular and ability groups. Many of the advantages of heterogeneous groups are traced to the high expectations, better behavior, and higher-quality teaching that occur when better students are present. These advantages reflect what many researchers refer to as school and classroom climates, and a large number of studies demonstrate how the norms and values within both schools and classrooms influence students' achievement.

We also reviewed literature regarding the relationship of school facilities and school and classroom size to student achievement. Some studies discount the validity of these relationships. Yet our review indicates that resources and, especially, the ways in which teachers allocate and link resources (including materials and time for learning) to individual students clearly influence the amount of learning that can take place. In addition, the size of the environment in which students learn, both classrooms and schools, affects their achievement. This occurs not just because students can have more individualized attention, and thus more teacher resources in smaller settings, but also because such smaller settings seem to promote more effective school and classroom climates.

Finally, we examined the relation of community environments to students' achievement. The literature in this area suggests that the neighborhood context of a school and the relationship between the school and parents and community members can influence student achievement. This occurs through decisions regarding resources as well as the quality and strength of their relationships and academically related expectations.

Many of the studies that we reviewed were relatively atheoretical. Although some used midrange theories or post hoc theoretical explanations to account for their findings, a surprisingly large number did not even include these limited attempts to account for the results. Despite the lack of theoretical writings reflected in this literature, there are broad, long-standing theoretical traditions in the social sciences, and particularly in sociology, that have dealt with issues of the relationship between individuals and their environments. Below, we review elements of these theories and show how these insights can be used to account for the results reviewed in earlier chapters. In the second part of this chapter, we suggest a conceptual framework that can be used to summarize these theoretical insights and provide a parsimonious and analytically useful organization of the research findings regarding environmental influences, which can be used by those interested in promoting more effective educational environments.

We believe that theories are central to developing better understandings of social situations. They help explain behavior in the current time and help predict behavior in new situations by providing guides, or road maps, that can help observers and participants make sense of their experiences. Theoretical explanations developed to deal just with experiences within schools may appear to be especially useful because of their specificity. We believe, however, that more general social theories can be of even greater utility. These general social theories have been developed to account for wide varieties of social behavior. By seeing how these theories can account for environmental influences on student learning, it becomes apparent that what happens in schools is generally not extraordinary but simply behavior that one would expect given the environmental situation. Once we can understand why behaviors exist, it is much easier to think about how they can be changed.

## Classical and Contemporary Theory

Some sociologists have concentrated their analyses on structural characteristics of groups, such as their size and heterogeneity, and how they affect relationships among individuals; we first review literature from this theoretical orientation. We then explore a much broader tradition in sociology that has dealt more directly and specifically with linkages between the micro level of social interactions and the macro level of structural relationships, including norms, values, and power relationships. Although the tradition has been relatively minor within the field as a whole, some psychologists have also addressed this issue, and we also examine their work. Finally, a number of organizational theorists have examined the school as a social organization, and we review some of this work.

It is impossible to convey the complexities and subtleties of each of the theoretical views described below in such a short review. Nor can we discuss all of the theorists who have contributed to these perspectives. Our intent, however, is not to provide a detailed overview of the theoretical notions involved in each perspective but instead to show how these various approaches have addressed the issues of the relationship between individual behavior and environmental situations. Throughout this discussion, we provide examples to show how these theories can help explain the findings reviewed in earlier chapters.

## GROUP SIZE AND HETEROGENEITY

Georg Simmel, one of the earliest sociologists, wrote extensively about how the size of groups and overlapping group memberships affect social life (Simmel 1908/1950, 1923/1955). Building upon this work, Peter Blau (1977; Blau and Schwartz 1984) developed a series of theoretical propositions that describe how the size of groups and their heterogeneity influence the probability of intergroup contact and social mobility.

Group characteristics may involve the distribution of any number of individual-level variables, including ones we mentioned in previous chapters such as socioeconomic status, ability, and achievement. Blau and Schwartz demonstrate, both theoretically and empirically, that in more heterogeneous groups, individuals are more likely to have contact and relationships with individuals who are unlike themselves. This can be seen graphically in Part A of Figure 5.1.

Suppose that the letters in Figure 5.1 represent individual characteristics of students in a classroom, such as socioeconomic status, measured ability, or racial and ethnic background. In classroom A, each student has a chance of 20/24, or a .83 probability, of having contacts with a student with a different background. In the more homogeneous classroom B, a student in the majority (X) has only a 4/24, or .17, probability of having contact with a student of a different background. A student in one of the groups in the minority (V, W, Y, or Z) can only have peers in other groups. Of the 300 possible dyadic relationships within each classroom, 250 in classroom A will involve students of different backgrounds while only 90 in classroom B will be heterogeneous in nature.

Therefore, in classrooms with students from a wide variety of socioeconomic backgrounds, the probability that a given student will be partnered with a student from a different background is quite high. Conversely, in a very homogeneous classroom, such as that depicted in Part B of Figure 5.1, except for the students in the minority, who have no peers with identical

| Classroom A | Classroom B |
| --- | --- |
| V W X Y Z | V X X X X |
| V W X Y Z | W X X X X |
| V W X Y Z | X X X X X |
| V W X Y Z | Y X X X X |
| V W X Y Z | Z X X X X |

**Figure 5.1.** Two Hypothetical Classrooms That Illustrate the Structural Effects of Group Composition

backgrounds, the probability that a student will be partnered with a student from a different background is very low. As Blau and Schwartz describe it, "structural conditions," in this case the heterogeneity of a classroom, "determine whether there will be extensive intergroup relations despite strong ingroup preferences or few intergroup relations even in areas where ingroup preferences are weak" (Blau and Schwartz 1984, p. 196). Figure 5.1 illustrates how students in classroom A have many more opportunities to interact with peers from a wide variety of backgrounds than do students in the much more homogeneous classroom B.

These structural conditions also influence the probability of individual mobility, or movement from one status to another. Associates in other groups or strata can facilitate the mobility of individuals into those groups. As more heterogeneous settings provide greater intergroup contact, they lay the basis for relationships that can provide the route to greater social mobility. Blau stresses that the more heterogeneity can penetrate into smaller subunits, then the greater is the probability that relationships between those from widely different status backgrounds will develop.

Blau and Schwartz (1984) test these theoretical notions using data on intermarriage and social mobility in a wide variety of cities in the United States, but the application to the literature regarding student groupings and achievement seems clear. Our discussion in Chapter 2 showed that students generally have higher achievement when they are in more heterogeneous learning situations—in desegregated schools, with higher-status students, and in classrooms that are not ability grouped or tracked. As Blau and Schwartz would suggest, heterogeneous grouping is most effective at the smallest subunits, as in cooperative learning groups within classrooms. In heterogeneous schools, classrooms, and groups, such as those in Part A of Figure 5.1, students are more likely to have contact with others from widely different social backgrounds and thus greater possibilities of developing relationships with individuals from backgrounds different from their own. This in turn can influence their self-views and their aspirations and result in greater chances of social mobility.

## THE MICRO-MACRO LINK

Blau's work and the formulations of Simmel were consciously limited to a macro level of analysis and focused only on characteristics such as size and heterogeneity. They avoided concepts such as values, norms, attitudes, and individual actions and did not try to explain the linkages between individuals' day-to-day actions and group characteristics. A much broader tradition of sociological work has dealt directly with these linkages between the macro level of social structure and the micro level of social interaction. In various ways, theorists in this tradition have tried to understand the relationship between individuals' understandings of and actions in their social situation and the maintenance of social order and predictability. They have tried to explain how individuals create their social world and how, in turn, this social world influences their individual actions.

The contemporary social theorist Jeffrey Alexander (1984, p. 6) has noted that "the most fundamental assumptions that inform any social-scientific theory concern the nature of action and order." Action generally involves what sociologists call a micro level of analysis. It includes individual acts and interactions, the day-to-day activities in which we all engage, the ways in which we communicate with others and plan and carry out our day-to-day activities. Order refers not just to structural characteristics such as group size and heterogeneity discussed above but also to group norms, expectations, values, and power relationships—all the elements and characteristics of social groups and interactions that allow us to maintain regular and patterned activities that are much the same from one day to the next.

Social order influences the actions that we take in our day-to-day lives, while everyday actions help both maintain and alter existing social orders. Figure 5.2 illustrates this relationship. The social order influences the nature of actions in two very basic ways: First, as individuals are "socialized" and come to accept and internalize group norms and values as their own, they behave in ways that are acceptable to the group. Second, various social control mechanisms can be used to compel individuals to behave in ways that conform with group expectations, a common response when individuals have not fully accepted the group's norms or values. Yet individuals do not simply blindly accept the social order or even social controls, and their own actions influence the nature of the social order or group characteristics. First, individuals legitimate group norms and values as they act in accordance with them and accept them as their own, and, without this continual legitimation, the social order would not continue to exist. Second, individuals may actively work against the existing social order through various modes of resistance and thus produce alterations and changes in the group's organization and norms and values.

To some extent, each of the three major classical sociological theorists—Émile Durkheim, Max Weber, and Karl Marx—addressed the linkage of social order and action and aspects of the relationships modeled in Figure 5.2. In later years, the issues resurfaced in the writings of Talcott Parsons and, most recently, in the work of Jeffrey Alexander and James Coleman. Below, we discuss aspects of these theoretical notions and show how they can be used to help explain some of the environmental influences on student achievement discussed in earlier chapters.

*Classical sociological theorists. Karl Marx*, the earliest of these writers, addressed the issue of the linkage between individual actions and the social structure most often in his early writings (e.g., Marx 1844/1963), although elements of these ideas persist in his later works. This tradition has been revised and used extensively by contemporary "critical theorists" (see Alexander 1984, pp. 10-14). In these writings, Marx focused not only upon how the situation in which an individual lives can greatly influence the course of his or her life but also upon how an

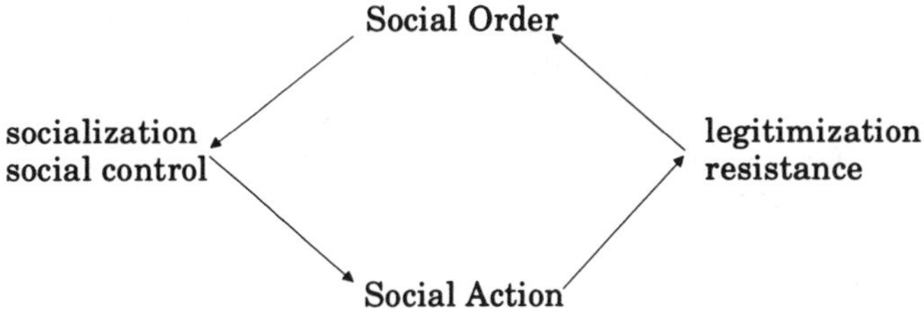


**Figure 5.2.** The Relationship Between Social Order and Social Action

individual creates his or her social situation and has the capacity to change it. Contemporary writers concerned with "Critical Pedagogy," such as Henry Giroux (1988a, 1988b) and Peter McLaren (1989), have been greatly influenced by the idea that individuals can have a transformative effect upon their social environment. They provide extensive examples of how teachers and students can provoke change within schools and within their lives through resisting oppressive structures.

A great deal of research attention has focused on students' resistance to teachers and schools, especially in the upper grades, and how students' reactions to the classroom and school can markedly affect school and classroom climate and student achievement. Students' behavior can vary widely within a school or classroom—from enthusiasm and devotion to schoolwork, to passive avoidance of assignments and school-related tasks, to active refusals to participate and dropping out of school all together (see Everhart 1983; Schofield 1982; Cusick 1983). These student behaviors are a key element of school and classroom climate, obviously reflecting and affecting student and teacher morale and the ability to maintain an orderly and academically oriented environment. Student behavior also affects teachers' and administrators' reactions and the choices they must make regarding allocation of resources, including personnel and time (Metz 1978; Cusick 1983). Sometimes parents' and community members' relationships with schools involve resistance. For instance, demands for community-controlled schools in inner-city, minority neighborhoods have often reflected parents' dissatisfaction with their children's schooling. Similarly, parents' reluctance to participate in school-related activities or to communicate openly with teachers may reflect their uneasiness with the school culture. Through these various actions, students and parents are resisting the nature of the school's social order and bringing about change.

*Émile Durkheim's* writings explore the linkages between individuals and their social structure more explicitly and thoroughly than Marx's. For instance, in *The Division of Labor in Society* (1933), Durkheim showed how the division of responsibilities among people within a society or a social group actually serves to bind them together, much as Simmel's and Blau's work demonstrated the effect of heterogeneity on patterns of relationships. This can also be seen in Barker and Gump's comparisons of small and large schools. Both small and large schools must perform similar functions, but in smaller schools fewer people are available to carry out the tasks and thus more people must be involved in and share the various activities. Through their greater involvement in the common enterprise, students in smaller schools are more attached to the group, have fewer behavior problems, and help create more effective school climates.

Durkheim's later writings went beyond his interest in the division of labor and concentrated on the normative structure of society, the *conscience collective.* He saw these norms as, in fact, a creation of individuals and a reflection of their own relations and of society itself (see especially Durkheim 1903/1961, 1912/1915). These normative structures are then internalized, or accepted, by individuals and used as guides and arbiters of future action. Although Marx's writings, especially his later works, focused on how the economic structure of the society influenced the "superstructure" of ideologies and values, Durkheim developed a complex view of the relationship between individuals and society that sees social order, the normative structure of a society, as both reflecting and influencing individuals.

Many observers of schools and classrooms have described the important role of an orderly and achievement-oriented environment in creating effective schools. These environments or "social orders" are most likely to occur when individuals accept or internalize the expectations of a group rather than when disciplinary procedures and auxiliary reinforcements must be continually used. In other words, orderliness results much more easily and effectively from students accepting and internalizing norms than from teachers imposing social controls. To understand this point, one can simply imagine two schoolrooms, both of which have skilled teachers who hold high academic expectations. In one classroom, students enter the room quietly, take out their work, and prepare to focus their attention on the teacher and their assignments even before the bell rings to signal the start of school. In the other classroom, there is a high noise level, students are engaged in social activities, and the teacher must remind them several times after the bell rings that it is time to begin work. Clearly, much more learning can occur within a classroom when students have internalized achievement-related norms and expectations of an orderly environment. Students in such a classroom are engaged in learning because they want to be, not just because someone tells them that they should or must.

*Max Weber,* the most recent of the three classic sociological theorists, contributed the notion of "legitimation," which he developed in his discussion of political power. Power can involve raw strength, but, for greatest effectiveness, it also needs to be accepted by individuals as legitimate. If power is accepted as legitimate, it has the force of strength as well as authority (Weber 1946, 1968). Much of the effective schools literature stresses the importance of orderly school and classroom environments and the role that principals can play as instructional leaders. In the example of the two classrooms given above, the students in the first classroom have legitimated the authority of the school and the teacher, while, in the second, they are actively resisting that authority. Clearly, achievement will be higher in schools where the social order is seen as legitimate by its members. Both principals and teachers can help influence the nature of school environments and the extent to which students and parents see them as legitimate.

More recently, educational theorists Svi Shapiro (1989) and Robert Young (1990) have used Jürgen Habermas's (1975, 1987) notion of "legitimation crisis" to argue that many current conflicts over schooling are related to the delegitimation of authority structures in the larger social world. They suggest that social institutions such as education were once granted authority based on "transcendent standards of ethical conduct or moral values" (Shapiro 1989, p. 19). Yet, in recent years, vast growth and changes in the technological and bureaucratic nature of society have undermined these traditional forms of authority and diminished the degree of control granted to institutional participants such as teachers, students, and parents. In other words, citizens may now be more likely to question the authority of traditional figures than they once were and to question school policies and programs. A more general "legitimation crisis" within the society at large may be reflected in the questioning or resistance displayed by parents and students in individual schools.

Much of the literature we have reviewed emphasizes the importance of establishing relationships between schools, community members, and parents that facilitate their involvement in both the educational process and policy formation. Likewise, the literature on effective schools highlights the importance of organizing schools in a manner that promotes cohesive relationships among a school's staff, teachers, and students. We believe that the success of educational reform programs is closely related to the extent to which they can demonstrate that they are democratically serving and responding to the educational goals and needs of all community members, parents, teachers, and students. This requires strong leadership of principals and teachers, but it also requires that their authority be seen as legitimate and accepted by all school constituents. The possibility that orderly schools will develop without extensive coercion and/or resistance is closely related to the extent to which the authority of school officials is legitimated in the eyes of students, teachers, parents, and community members (see Metz 1978; Grant 1982).

*Functionalism.* Beginning in the 1930s, Talcott Parsons used the writings of Durkheim and, to some extent, Weber to develop his wide-ranging theoretical views, generally known as structural functionalism. Parsons dealt explicitly with questions of action and order. His work, and that of other functionalists, is centrally concerned with the question of social integration: how social order develops. In this analysis, he simply assumes that deviance, or resistance, and social control will exist in a social group (Alexander 1985, pp. 9-10; see also Stevenson 1991). Legitimation is seen as "the primary link between values . . . of the individual and the institutionalized patterns which define the structure of social relationships" (Parsons 1960, p. 175).

Parsons and other structural functionalists stress the multilevel nature of the social world—the distinction between individual personalities, social situations, and cultural influences and the interpenetration of these levels of analysis.

Functionalists suggest that individuals interpret and evaluate social situations in terms of their relevance to various "goals, interests and normative standards" (Devereux 1961, p. 22). In Parsons's view, a "social system" develops whenever two or more people have some type of stable, patterned mode of interaction. In his work with R. F. Bales, Parsons came to suggest that any social system faces certain functional problems or issues. Some deal with the relation of the social system to the external environment and goal attainment, and some deal with conditions internal to the social system. These eventually became known as the instrumental-expressive distinction. Instrumental actions concern the attainment of group goals and relationships of the social system to the external situation; expressive actions deal with the relationships among actors within a social system and the maintenance of cohesion and motivation. Both types of actions are goal oriented and essential to the maintenance of the social system; they are simply oriented toward different types of goals (Parsons and Shils 1952; Parsons et al. 1954; Devereux 1961). In his studies of leadership in small groups, Bales noted the importance of leadership activities directed toward both instrumental and expressive activities. Sometimes a group will have both a leader who focuses on instrumental activities and one who focuses on expressive activities; other times, one person will be both the expressive and the instrumental leader (Bales 1950).

Schools and classrooms may be seen as social systems with a social order that is legitimated and, at times, resisted by its participants (see Parsons 1958, 1959). Wayne Hoy and his associates have used Parsons's and Bales's formulations as a basis for describing the characteristics of healthy schools. As they put it, "Healthy schools effectively meet the instrumental needs of adaptation and goal achievement as well as the expressive needs of social and normative integration; that is, they must mobilize their resources to achieve their goals as well as infuse common values into the work group" (Hoy et al. 1991, p. 68). The literature we reviewed in previous chapters provides clear support for this interpretation. The social and normative integration that comes from meeting expressive needs of a group raises the morale of individuals and helps influence group members to accept and legitimate group norms, thus minimizing the need for more formal means of social control. Establishing high-achievement-related norms, or meeting instrumental needs, helps ensure that group energies are directed toward productive tasks rather than other endeavors. The most effective principals and teachers are those who can incorporate both instrumental and expressive orientations into their leadership style—encouraging high-achievement-related norms while promoting high morale and feelings of inclusion. Both aspects are crucial for successful schools (see Good and Brophy 1986, p. 596; Cohen 1983; Grant 1982; Halpin 1966, p. 170; Hoy et al. 1991, pp. 139, 150; Bossert 1988b, p. 346).

For a number of years, especially from the mid-1960s through the early 1970s, the writings of structural functionalists were heavily criticized for their supposed conservative, anti-individualist, and antiempirical bias. More recently, however, a growing number of social theorists have returned to the writings of functionalist theorists, including Parsons. They have expanded upon this work, often incorporating insights from other theoretical traditions including Marxism and the broader range of conflict theory as well as elements of economic and social-psychological theories (see Sciulli and Gerstein 1985; Alexander and Giesen 1987; Alexander 1982a, 1982b, 1983a, 1983b, 1985). This work has explicitly focused on individual actions and their linkage to the social order.

*Neofunctionalism.* Jeffrey Alexander has been the major developer and proponent of "neofunctionalism" and has probably done more to resurrect Parsons's image and integrate his work with other theoretical traditions than any other contemporary theorist. He shows how Parsons's work can be seen as a general framework that deals with the central issues of order and action and that other theoretical traditions can be used to complement and fill out this framework. For instance, the various micro theories of social interaction, such as exchange theory, ethnomethodology, phenomenology, and symbolic interaction, can be used to explain different aspects of what Parsons referred to as a social "act." Exchange theory, based on the work of George Homans (1961), can explain the "contingency" of actions, how material conditions affect individual choices. The factors that influence distribution of these material conditions can be described by Marxism and other conflict theories. Ethnomethodology and phenomenology (e.g., Garfinkel 1967) can help explain the continuity and pattern of social interactions, while symbolic interaction (Blumer 1969) can explain the effect of immediate interactions on individuals' interpretations of events and their subsequent actions. In general, these theories can be important in helping spell out how and why students, teachers, and parents choose certain types of actions within their classrooms or schools.

Alexander has devoted a great deal of attention to using these ideas to elaborate and flesh out Parsons's notion of "action." The concept of contingency is central to this theoretical work. Building on the insights of conflict theorists, such as Marx, and exchange theorists, such as Homans, Alexander notes that all actions involve both interpretation and strategization. In much the same way that psychologists discuss cognitive "schemas," Alexander suggests that individuals interpret the world by "typifying" or categorizing experiences but also by "inventing" explanations and understandings. Strategization involves what critical theorists have called "praxis" (Marx 1845/1965): intentional, goal-related action that involves "not merely understanding the world, [but] also transforming and acting upon it" (Alexander 1987, p. 302).

This work shows how individuals are not automatons, responding blindly to social controls or their internalization of norms. Instead, social action involves individual choice: Students choose how they will behave in a class; teachers choose how they will allocate their time and materials; administrators choose how they will respond to students or parents. These choices are, of course, influenced by the nature of the school environment and individuals' own social background. Individuals' actions are very much influenced by the material and social conditions in which they find themselves. Students and teachers in poor communities with few resources and large, crowded schools clearly have different options than those in smaller schools with more resources and a different community environment. Thus social environments influence actions—both by constraint and by inspiration. Simultaneously, however, actions create social environments. Individuals interpret the worlds in which they interact and strategize or choose the actions they will take. This occurs in all social settings. We believe that environments can be created in all kinds of schools that will help facilitate choices and actions by students, parents, and teachers that will be most conducive to high achievement.

James Coleman's theoretical work (1986a, 1986b, 1988, 1990) can directly address how this might be accomplished. In Chapter 4, we introduced his notion of "social capital" and the idea that human actors create social capital: the relationships among individuals that provide a supportive environment for children. He stresses that social capital is "an important resource for individuals and may affect greatly their ability to act and their perceived quality of life" (Coleman 1988, p. S118). Communities and schools differ in the extent to which they promote social capital, and evidence from the work of Coleman and others suggests that these variations can help explain the differential effectiveness of schools in different communities.

Coleman suggests that we can conceive of individuals in a social setting as rational, goal-directed actors. Building upon the notion of utility maximization of economists and the public choice work that is more common in political science, he suggests that individuals calculate (or "strategize," in Alexander's terminology) the relative costs and benefits of pursuing various goals or participating in some group effort. These choices are not just influenced by individual actors trying to maximize their own selfish benefits but are also influenced by feelings of trust and emotional ties. In addition, other variables surrounding a situation, what Alexander refers to as "contingencies," can influence the choices and actions that individuals take (Coleman 1986a, 1986b, 1987b, 1990).

This implies that, if students, parents, teachers, and administrators are going to choose to work together to create more effective school environments, their chances of doing so would be greatly improved if they believed that the benefits of doing so would outweigh the costs. The benefits may include not just long-range goals of economic success that can result from higher achievements but more subjective benefits of association and supportive relationships with other people as well as simply the inherent satisfactions that can arise from the intellectual accomplishments of teaching and learning. When actors within schools and classrooms—including students, parents, teachers, and administrators—come to believe that they, whether as individuals or family units, will benefit from the efforts required to work together to develop more effective classrooms, then it is much more likely that they will succeed. The challenge for those interested in promoting these efforts is developing incentives that are meaningful for all participants.

## THE MICRO-MACRO LINK IN PSYCHOLOGY

Although the tradition is much smaller, some psychologists have also addressed the issue of linkages between individual behavior and the environment. Much of this work has been influenced by Kurt Lewin (e.g., 1935, 1951) and the general area known as "field theory," as well as by Henry Murray's (1938) work on "environmental press." Although Lewin and other field researchers used the term *structures* to refer to cognitive structures or schemas, and not the macro structures that many sociologists refer to, they explicitly recognized the influence of the group environment on individuals' behavior. They assert that human behavior cannot be understood apart from the environment in which it occurs and that both the physical and the social environment must be studied in understanding these effects. Much of this work has an explicit applied orientation, with a goal of developing more optimal environments for individuals (Moos and Insel 1974, p. x). The work of Roger Barker and Rudolf Moos illustrates this tradition of psychological work and directly relates to material reviewed in earlier chapters.

*Social ecology and undermanning theory.* Roger Barker and his colleagues at the University of Kansas have conducted many studies on the relation between human behavior and the environment in which it occurs, and Barker refers to himself as an "eco-behavioral scientist" (Barker 1978, p. 285; see also Barker 1968; Barker and Gump 1964; Barker et al. 1978; Wicker 1973). Building on some of Lewin's concepts, Barker and his colleagues use the notion of a "behavior setting" to define the environment in which behavior occurs. Not unlike Parsons's emphasis on the importance of looking at different levels of analysis, Barker emphasizes that behaviors can be fully understood only when they are examined within the context in which they occur.

An important outgrowth of this work is "undermanning theory." According to this theory, all behavior settings have a certain number of essential functions or tasks. When there are too few people or barely enough people to carry out these tasks, the continuance of the setting is threatened and pressures are engendered on the occupants to help maintain it. In other words, "the *claim* of the behavior setting on its inhabitants is greater in conditions of undermanning than when the number of persons available is at or above the optimal level" (Wicker 1973, p. 187, emphasis in original).

This theory was first developed through research on small schools, in which Barker and his colleague Paul Gump studied 13 secondary schools that varied in enrollment from 35 to more than 2,000 students. As we noted in Chapter 4, they and other researchers have found that smaller schools must carry on many of the same activities and functions that larger schools do without as many people to fulfill the needed tasks. Thus students in smaller schools, especially those with marginal academic ability, are much more likely to be pulled into school activities and to feel more committed and obligated to their schools than are similar students in larger schools. Barker and Gump and their colleagues and students have replicated these results in a number of other settings. Just as Durkheim's analysis of the division of labor noted how the partialing of tasks among group members helps to bind them to each other, Barker and Gump's analysis indicates how the size of a group relative to the tasks that need to be completed can be a very important factor in binding group members to the group as a whole. It also implies that those interested in designing effective schools where students, staff, and parents are more committed to and involved with the school mission would do well to pay attention to the size of the school.

*Social ecology and organizational climates.* Although Barker focused on the effects of group size on individuals' behavior, Rudolf Moos and his colleagues have explored how perceptions of the "climate" of a situation, such as an organization, a classroom, or a school, influence people's behaviors and ties to the group. This work has been inspired by Henry Murray's (1938) work on "environmental press" and the notion that the environments in which individuals interact can be seen as having characteristics or a "personality" of their own (see Moos 1976). Over the years, they have done a great deal of work developing scales to measure individuals' perceptions of their environments. These scales often can be lengthy and complex yet yield remarkably complete pictures of group members' views of their environments. As we noted in our discussion of school and classroom climates, teachers who work in settings that they perceive are more supportive tend to be happier in their work and to do a better job. In addition, students who perceive that classrooms are more orderly and goal oriented, yet interpersonally supportive, tend to have higher achievement (e.g., Moos 1979; Hoy et al. 1991).

Some research has also dealt with the question of the fit between a person and the environment: the congruence between individuals' personality characteristics and the settings in which they live and work. Some of the earliest work on school climates focused on the fit between the leadership styles of school principals and the climates of their schools as perceived by the teaching staff (e.g., Halpin and Croft 1962). This work suggests that the most effective schools are those that have an "open" climate, where both the principal and the faculty are "genuine and open in their interactions," where teachers and the principal are committed to their tasks, and where the entire staff works well together without close supervision, excessive paperwork, or extensive and impersonal rules. The least effective schools are those with a "closed" climate, where routine trivia are stressed; neither faculty nor the principal indicates commitment to their work; and low morale is commonplace (Hoy et al. 1991, pp. 15-16). Studies of school climate seem to suggest that no one leadership style will be effective in all schools. That is, there is no prescribed pattern for developing an open climate in all schools. As Hoy and his colleagues suggest, "The patterns of principal and teacher behavior work together to ensure commitment; leadership patterns of the principal must complement the interaction patterns of teachers" (Hoy et al. 1991, p. 140).

The emphasis on the relationship between individual and environmental characteristics can also apply to analyses of the fit between students and their schools and classrooms. The way in which congruence between the person and the environment affects individual behavior may well depend on the nature of both individual characteristics and the environment (Moos 1987). For instance, work on the relationship between home and school clearly indicates that student achievement is enhanced when parents and teachers hold common expectations regarding academic behavior. Similarly, when students who hold high academic expectations and tend to be very task oriented are in a task-oriented environment, they may prosper. In other circumstances, a close person-environment fit may not be productive. For instance, students who come from homes that provide little academic or socioemotional support are probably not helped by being in nonacademically oriented or emotionally unsupportive settings.

In general, work coming out of psychological traditions does not contradict the general thrust of sociological theories regarding the relationship between individuals and their environments. Although the work of Barker and his colleagues can be seen as enhancing our knowledge of how group characteristics, and particularly group size, affect individuals' behavior and group characteristics, the work of Moos and others on organizational climates provides insights into individuals' perceptions of social groups and how these influence the ways in which they make decisions about actions and their interactions with others within the group. Yet another theoretical tradition that looks at the link between individuals and their environments is work that focuses specifically on social organizations.

## THE SCHOOL AS A SOCIAL ORGANIZATION

A large number of theorists have examined the school as a social organization and its relation to learning. Some analysts have dealt primarily with global issues, such as the function of education, describing how it serves to reproduce the class structure (e.g., Bowles and Gintis 1976) or to credential individuals and restrict access to higher-status occupational areas (e.g., Collins 1979). Others have looked at schools in a slightly less far-reaching, yet still widely applicable, manner, focusing on the actual organizational characteristics of schools. These analyses help point out how specific organizational characteristics of schools and classrooms can be related to student achievement.

For instance, John Meyer (1980) suggests that it is important to study institutional categories of education—such as grade levels, types of schools, and areas of study. When one views education in this institutional framework, it is obvious that schools greatly affect students' lives. Students learn different things in fourth grade than in third grade and know much more at the end of fourth grade than at the end of third grade. Similarly, students who have a high school diploma have a much greater chance of occupational success than those who do not. This is true no matter what the quality of a school that a student might graduate from or the quality of the education that a dropout may have obtained prior to leaving school. According to Meyer, these and other institutionalized aspects of education are very standard at least across the United States.

He suggests that students may be seen as rational actors who negotiate this institutional structure of education, making choices about their commitment to the student role. Teachers and administrators may also be seen as rational actors (in Coleman's terms) or as using strategies (in Alexander's terms) to best accomplish institutional goals. Whether it is a teacher deciding how to cover the material that should be taught in third grade or a principal ensuring that a high school has all of the courses necessary to retain certification, developing strategies to meet these institutional requirements is necessary to maintain organizational credibility (Meyer 1980; also Meyer and Rowan 1977, 1978).

Despite these uniformities in educational institutions, schools themselves are often described as organizations that are "loosely coupled" (Weick 1976). That is, within schools, teachers have a great deal of discretion and independence in the ways they may choose to structure their classes and teach their students. Even as schools have become increasingly more bureaucratized and standardized (e.g., Tyack 1974), teachers and other school personnel have retained extensive freedom in the way they conduct their classes. At the same time, this loose coupling works against close collegial relations between teachers, so that it can be rare for teachers to collaborate with each other or share problems they may be having (see McPherson 1972; Rosenholtz 1989), even though they are working toward common institutional goals. Some schools have increased teacher collegiality and communication and tried to modify the loose coupling of the organization while retaining a professional orientation toward teachers. Notably, teachers in these schools are both more satisfied with their work and more effective instructors (Rosenholtz 1989). A major challenge for those seeking to develop effective schools is determining ways to enhance supportive and collegial relationships among teachers without losing the advantages of loosely coupled organizations and without sacrificing efforts to meet a variety of institutional requirements.

Some theorists have also looked at the classroom as an organization. In an article titled "The School Class as a Social System," Talcott Parsons (1959) contrasts the organization and goals of the classroom to those of the family. He notes that, although the school is concerned with universalistic and achievement norms, the family has particularistic norms regarding a child. These are functional for the child and the society in general as children move from the insular world of the family to the achievement-oriented adult world. As we noted in Chapter 5, however, these different orientations can result in conflicts between parents and teachers that sometimes seem almost insurmountable (McPherson 1972; Lightfoot 1978). Coming from the tradition called the "New Sociology of Education," some theorists have discussed ways in which classroom procedures and processes perpetuate social inequalities and actually prevent many students, especially those whose characteristics differ from those of the teachers, from achieving all that they might (e.g., Giroux 1983; Apple 1982, 1988; see also Alexander et al. 1987). In an analysis that echoes insights of the neofunctionalists, these theorists suggest that schools, through social control mechanisms, may have repressive effects on students, but also that students may resist or act against these repressive situations in an attempt to gain their own personal goals, such as the maintenance of self-esteem. Just as the neofunctionalists have tried to integrate understandings of individual actions with analyses of social control and legitimation, some organizational theorists have stressed the importance of understanding how students' and teachers' actions affect organizational structures (e.g., Tyler 1985).

Finally, some theorists have dealt directly with the issue of school effectiveness and schools as organizations, introducing important conceptual clarifications. Charles Bidwell and John Kasarda (1980) suggest that the school effects literature has confused schools as social organizations with schooling, the process through which instruction occurs. Schooling as an organizational process involves the many organizational decisions that affect students' experiences in schools such as the division of students into ability groups, tracks, or even segregated schools and the distribution of resources such as time and materials. It is schooling, the human decisions and actions, that affect achievement, much more than schools as organizations and their aggregate resources (see also Barr and Dreeben 1983, 1985; Levin 1980; and the discussion in Chapter 3). Thus, in their own way, these organizational theorists are stressing the importance of social action—the choices and decisions of individuals within school organizations—in determining how effective a given school may become.

## SUMMARY

Despite their varying underlying orientations and disciplinary roots, the theories briefly described above share common themes in explaining the relationship between social environments and human behavior. First, it seems clear from these analyses that the nature of a group in which people interact, whether it is a society, a community, or an organization such as a school, influences people's behaviors and attitudes. This influence is analytically distinct from the influence of an individual's own background and characteristics. In other words, the same individual may behave quite differently in different groups and different social settings. A given child may have totally different experiences and achievement in one school or classroom than in another, even though his or her family background and intellectual capabilities remain unchanged.

Second, all of the theories reviewed recognize that understandings of human behavior need to be multilevel in nature. It is not enough simply to analyze individuals' behaviors and actions apart from the environment in which they exist. Similarly, it is not sufficient simply to analyze organizational characteristics and relationships apart from the experiences of the individuals involved in those groups. Complex, multilevel, integrative analyses are crucial. Full analyses of student achievement must include attention not just to individuals' characteristics such as their ability and family background but also to the nature of their classrooms, schools, and communities.

Third, many of the theories specifically address the interactive relationship between social order and social action. Social order may be conceived in a variety of ways, including norms and values, environmental climate, or aspects of the organizational structure. Social action does not involve blind reactions to a larger social structure but instead involves calculating, thoughtful responses of reasoning human beings to the social order in which they live. Social order, however it is conceived, serves to bind group members to each other, is a guide for both group and individual behavior (Durkheim, Parsons, Alexander, Moos, Meyer), and is internalized by individuals through a process of socialization. At the same time, the social order is continually created and developed by the social actions, the day-to-day decisions, of individuals (Coleman, Alexander, Marx). For an authority or social order to be accepted, individuals must see it as legitimate, and actions that are reflective of the social order help to support and maintain it, through what is called a process of legitimation (Parsons, Weber). When individuals do not accept the social order and/or when the authority it represents is overly repressive, resistance to the order may occur, and the social order alters in response to these actions (Marx, Giroux, Alexander). Schools and classrooms may be seen as social orders that directly affect the lives of students, teachers, and parents; yet, through their daily actions, these individuals reinforce and alter this existing social order.

Finally, all of these relationships are contingent on various social conditions. For instance, the size and heterogeneity of groups confine and determine the extensiveness of relationships that may develop and the extent to which individuals must actively participate in group activities. Individuals' and organizations' access to resources affect the range of decisions that are possible for them to make. Institutional requirements and organizational structures influence the types of interactions that people can have and limit the nature of actions that individuals can choose. Group members' interpersonal relations and emotional feelings of trust affect the nature of their interactions (Parsons, Alexander, Blau, Coleman, and Barker and Gump). Thus small schools in rural communities where teachers and parents have long-standing relationships with each other may face very different issues in developing effective schools than do larger schools in urban areas with long histories of antagonisms between parents and school staff.

## A Conceptual Framework for Understanding Effective Educational Environments

It is clear from the discussion above that social theorists from several fields have spent a good deal of effort describing the relationship between social environments and individuals' experiences. We have attempted to show how these analyses can help explain some of the findings discussed in earlier chapters regarding environmental influences on student achievement and how these influences may be understood in much the same way as environmental influences on other types of behavior. In other words, general theories from sociology, psychology, and the study of organizations can account for environmental influences on students' learning as well as many other types of behavior.

Taken separately, the extensive theoretical writings referred to above may help inform researchers interested in specific aspects of environmental influences. Yet they may not be especially usable for teachers, parents, policymakers, and administrators who are concerned with the day-to-day aspects of developing more effective schools and classrooms. Practitioners might be better served by a relatively parsimonious development, which incorporates these varied theoretical insights and can serve as a guide for changes in educational environments yet maintain the flexibility that would encourage its use in a variety of settings.

In earlier chapters, we reviewed literature on four key areas of environmental influences on student achievement—student groupings, learning climates, school facilities and size, and the community. Building on the theoretical traditions reviewed above, we suggest that it is possible to integrate these influences within the two broad-ranging concepts of *social order* and *social action*, which are found to some extent in all of the theories reviewed above. Within the concept of social order, we include all the various aspects of social life that reflect patterned, regularized activities: norms and values of a group; a group's climate or culture; and its organizational structure, including its institutional mission and assigned roles. Within the concept of social action, we include all the various aspects related to individuals' actions and interactions: their social relations, their legitimation of and resistance to the social order, their implementation of social control mechanisms, and their strategization and choices in their day-to-day lives. The social order defines acceptable behavior within a group; social actions influence the extent to which individuals are tied into the group and either accept and legitimate or resist and try to alter the existing social order.

We also suggest that the nature of social order and social action can be further specified by considering their "instrumental" and "expressive" orientations. Based on the literature reviewed in earlier chapters, we suggest that effective schools and classrooms need to develop social orders that incorporate an appropriate balance of both achievement-oriented instrumental norms and emotionally supportive expressive norms. In addition, the relationships among individuals that produce social actions need to include activities that are directed toward both expressive- and instrumental-related goals. Both types of orientations are crucial for school success. Instrumental orientations provide the impetus and means for stressing and maintaining high achievement goals and expectations. Expressive orientations provide the basis for high morale and feelings of inclusion by all school participants.

Taken together, we believe that these concepts provide a parsimonious framework in which to analyze activities that occur in schools as well as the relative balance and frequency of these activities as they differ from school to school. We realize that this framework is quite simple, especially in light of the rather complex listings of variables often found in models of student achievement (e.g., Centra and Potter 1980; Harnischfeger and Wiley 1980). Such elaborate models may be extremely informative in summarizing the literature and suggesting specific hypotheses for further research. Yet, in their complexity, we believe that they may not be especially useful to practitioners. Moreover, they can disguise a very consistent theme in the literature: Student achievement is enhanced by positive instrumental norms—those stressing academic goals, persistence, and high expectations for students—and positive expressive norms—those involving supportive, humane relationships. The extent to which such normative orders can be developed and accepted within a school is a product of social action, that is, individual choices that are influenced by the relationships among school members. We believe that most of the literature dealing with environmental influences on student achievement can be subsumed within this overriding conceptual view and that it can provide a useful framework for practitioners interested in developing effective educational environments in a wide variety of settings as well as scholars searching for a parsimonious explanation of the vast variety of influences on student achievement.

## EFFECTIVE SOCIAL ORDERS FOR SCHOOLS

In describing the social order of educational environments, we focus on *norms* and *values,* for these terms can incorporate most aspects of school climates or cultures as well as a group's assigned missions and roles. A number of authors have used concepts first developed by Talcott Parsons and his associates (Parsons and Shils 1952; Parsons et al. 1954) to analyze schools as social orders (e.g., Shipman 1968; Hoy et al. 1991). These authors suggest that the ongoing activities of a school involve both instrumental activities, those oriented toward task completion, and expressive activities, those oriented toward promoting socioemotional integration of the group. One may talk about both norms and values that are related to these instrumental and expressive activities. Although both types of activities may be seen within classrooms and schools, the relative balance and frequency of these actions may differ from one school to another, and the research reviewed in earlier chapters stresses that both types of norms are essential to developing effective educational environments.

As we noted above, instrumental activities are those that involve the attainment of learning goals: the actual work of learning. The literature suggests that learning groups that include more students from higher-status and higher-ability backgrounds more often have instrumental norms that support achievement and academic work. The literature on learning climates stresses the importance of instrumental norms in enhancing achievement. These instrumental aspects of effective schools and classrooms involve an emphasis on academic achievement, on learning basic skills, and on effective instructional leadership and teaching skills. The most effective teachers and administrators are those who expect high achievement and provide classroom environments that facilitate students' greater on-task behavior. Research related to school facilities suggests that providing adequate school resources and teacher training helps promote student achievement. School size and heterogeneity also affect instrumental norms: Smaller schools and classrooms and more heterogeneous groups seem better able to maintain achievement-oriented goals among all students, especially those who are more at risk of failure. In addition, literature suggests that better use of school resources (the more effective implementation of instrumental activities) may occur more often in small- to medium-sized schools than in larger schools (Eberts, Kehoe, et al. 1983; Eberts, Schwartz, et al. 1990).

Expressive activities are those that are related to the socioemotional atmosphere of the school and classroom; they might best be seen as promoting positive ties of students to school and the feelings of self-efficacy and locus of control that underlie achievement. The literature on student grouping indicates that students, especially those whose individual characteristics would suggest that they are at greater risk of academic failure, are generally more likely to have positive attitudes toward school and their own capabilities as well as higher achievement when they are in heterogeneous ability, racial, and socioeconomic groups. The literature on school climate notes the extent to which a warm and supportive environment, both among staff and between students and staff, can promote learning. The literature on school size suggests that the negative effect of greater school size on student achievement can be explained by the alienation and lack of interpersonal involvement and caring, as well as by the less orderly environments that more often appear in larger schools. Similarly, studies of the relationship between community environments and student achievement imply that more compatible, cohesive relationships between school staff, parents, and community members are associated with better attitudes toward school and higher student achievement.

Thus the literature suggests that having a social order within schools and classrooms that stresses both expressive and instrumental norms is a crucial aspect of environments that promote student achievement. Important instrumental, or task-related, norms involve expectations of high academic success and task orientation. Important expressive, or socioemotional-related, norms involve a supportive and caring atmosphere for students as well as staff.

## EFFECTIVE SOCIAL ACTIONS IN SCHOOLS

Simply distinguishing the types of activities that make up an effective school environment does not describe how individuals come to accept and participate in this social order or the ways in which the balance of various types of norms is determined. This involves *social action,* which reflects the relationships that group members have with each other and their choices and decisions within the group. The process of learning the norms associated with various social roles in a social order is commonly termed *socialization.* Analyses of socialization from a traditional functionalist perspective in sociology generally examine the sanctions or social control mechanisms used to encourage the display of behavior defined as appropriate and the ways in which definitions of appropriate behavior are conveyed among group members. As individuals accept the existing norms or social order and act in ways that conform to it, they reinforce or legitimate these norms. (See Parsons 1959; Jackson 1968; Dreeben 1973, for examples of this analysis within classrooms.) The literature reviewed above suggests that the most effective schools and classrooms are those in which participants tend to agree upon and accept, or legitimate, a social order that emphasizes high achievement. In these schools, the actions of students, teachers, parents, and administrators support this social order with a minimum of friction and disagreement and in an atmosphere of mutual support.

Unfortunately, many schools do not embody these characteristics. A more realistic picture of schools must note, as the neofunctionalists and conflict theorists do, that schools and other groups inherently involve coercion, conflicts, and contradictions. Both the heterogeneous background characteristics of students and staff and the compulsory nature of schooling contribute to the probability that members of a school will not accept and/or adhere to official norms and values of the school to the same degree (see Shipman 1968; Waller 1932; Giroux 1983; Willis 1977). Thus, within a school, students and staff will display various degrees of accommodation and resistance to the officially established norms and values. In addition, the actual norms and values found within a school (in contrast to those that are officially decreed) are themselves probably the product of continuous negotiation and renegotiation by group members: the process of social action. Thus the existence and maintenance of the social order depends on social actions, that is, the relationships among those within the group and the choices and decisions that group members make. Effective schools are those where students, parents, teachers, and administrators can work together in an atmosphere of mutual respect to develop group relationships that result in high academic expectations and agreed-upon ways of meeting achievement-related goals.

Thus the relations among group members influence the extent to which coercion, conflict, and patterns of resistance permeate and typify a school. For instance, the literature on learning climates suggests that safe and orderly environments promote learning. This may occur because such an environment is associated with relationships that are conducive to the acceptance or legitimation of common school norms. The literature on school size stresses the greater interdependence and closer ties among school members that appear in smaller schools. It appears that these are related to the lower levels of disciplinary problems and vandalism found in small schools and a safer, more orderly environment as well as one in which students and staff find more interpersonal support. The literature on the relationships between community environments and schools also relates directly to this issue. It suggests that schools with greater rapport between parents or community members and school staff have students with more favorable attitudes toward school and higher achievement. Such environments promote what James Coleman (1988) calls "social capital," atmospheres where students experience consistent expectations, clear and concise behavioral guidelines, and a strong network of adults who care about them and their achievement (see Coleman and Hoffer 1987). In general, we suggest that, when relationships between school members embody trust, rapport, and mutual understanding, an integrated and cohesive schooling structure is much more likely to appear. This in turn influences the extent to which those within a school can develop and legitimate norms supportive of academic achievement.

It must be remembered that students enter kindergarten and first grade with vastly different stores of knowledge, with different individual resources, and with different amounts of social capital. These differences remain and can even widen during the school career. Thus, within any one school or classroom, there can be great variability among the students and their parents in their attitudes toward the school and their ability to negotiate and participate with school staff members. Correspondingly, some parents and staff might be more likely to resist a school's normative order than others. We have emphasized that heterogeneous learning groups are important for developing more effective educational environments. Within such groups, however, it is essential that all parents and children, regardless of their capabilities or background characteristics, are treated with equal respect if maximum benefits are to be achieved.

In general, we believe that it is important to remember that students may have varying degrees of attachment to schools and that analyses of social action within schools need to incorporate notions of resistance as well as legitimation. With this analysis, we do not mean to imply, however, that schools in which there is little agreement on school norms or attachment to the officially sanctioned norms have little hope for academic success or that these academic benefits accrue equally to all children within a school. Nor do we wish to imply that "consensus" or "legitimation" is reflected by a member's compliance or acquiescence to officially sanctioned norms. Schools where dissension may not be apparent are not necessarily schools with the freely developed legitimation implied by the traditional functionalist model. Rather, compliance with school norms may be achieved through the imposition of authoritarian mechanisms. It is important to recognize that dissension may exist and that the basis of that conflict needs to be determined if achievement is to be enhanced. Given the heterogeneous characteristics of school members in most schools, resistance to officially sanctioned norms should be expected. We would hypothesize that resistance to school norms is most likely to emerge among disenfranchised sectors of a school's population precisely because they and their parents are least likely to be considered and/or involved in the development and maintenance of these norms. If learning is to be promoted among *all* children, resistance among disenfranchised members may well be seen as a positive rather than negative occurrence.

The task for researchers, as well as school officials, is understanding why this resistance appears and how it may be adequately addressed to allow academic benefits to accrue equally among all groups of children. We believe that a potentially fruitful way to examine this area is through detailing the association between relationships among members of a school and the nature of group values and norms, through examining the existing social order and social actions and their relative balance of instrumental and expressive orientations. Situations need to be created that enhance the probability that administrators, policymakers, teachers, students, and parents can create social orders that influence higher achievement. In the next chapter, we discuss specific policies that can help promote this goal.

# 6

# Policy and Research Directions

Throughout this book, we have asserted that the environments in which students learn can make a difference in their academic achievement. We have used long-standing theoretical traditions within the social sciences to integrate these findings into a simple, yet inclusive, framework. This framework suggests that the social order—group norms and values—and actions of individuals within the group—their relationships and choices—affect the extent to which an educational environment can effectively enhance students' learning.

We chose to focus on educational environments precisely because these are areas that are most amenable to change by policymakers. Below, we discuss policy implications of our analysis and provide suggestions for future research that can help further explicate some of the relationships discussed here. The policy changes we suggest involve concrete actions that policymakers, teachers, and administrators can take to facilitate the development of social orders that are more conducive to high achievement.

## Student Groupings

Our discussion in Chapter 1 focused on the effect of student groupings on achievement. It seems clear from this review that more heterogeneous groups generally tend to enhance student learning. Minority students in desegregated schools and lower-status children in schools with higher-status children tend to have higher achievement. Similarly, lower-ability students learn more when they are not in lower tracks or in low-ability groups. The major exception involves gender segregation, where girls and minority boys do better in single-sex schools, although majority boys do better in mixed-sex schools. This would imply that effective educational environments would be desegregated across race and ethnicity, social class, and ability levels. This desegregation should occur across schools within a district, within schools, and within classrooms.

### HETEROGENEOUS LEARNING GROUPS

Policy directed at racial desegregation has produced what can only be described as partial success in the last quarter century, with schools virtually as segregated now as they were a number of years ago. Christine Rossell has studied school desegregation efforts for a number of years. She recently concluded (Rossell 1990) that the most effective way to promote school desegregation is to establish high-quality magnet schools in minority neighborhoods. Magnet schools generally have special programs and resources, such as drama or science, and open enrollment policies in the hopes of attracting a wide range of students. When established in minority neighborhoods, the magnet programs both enhance the quality of the neighborhood school in which they are housed and help to desegregate the school by attracting nonminority children (Bastian et al. 1986). Magnet schools tend to have more satisfied and involved parents, an important element in enhancing student achievement. When used as a means for desegregation, Rossell contends that magnet schools result in less resistance and greater participation by members of the white majority than occurs with other mechanisms, such as bussing plans. In developing this suggestion, Rossell assumes that parents behave as rational actors, much as Coleman, Alexander, and Meyer describe, in choosing school environments for their children.[1]

Ending tracking procedures within schools involves decisions by teachers, administrators, parents, and students. Resistance to such a practice may well occur from the most privileged, who may fear that they will lose in the process. One way to counter these fears is to incorporate an end to school tracking with a redesign of schools into smaller units, essentially creating smaller schools, through such concepts as the "school within a school" or alternative schools. Tracking arose primarily as one way to handle masses of students in a comprehensive high school; if there are no longer masses of students, the need for tracking becomes less obvious. All students could have access to a common curriculum. Moreover, the literature suggests that students in all ability levels would benefit from learning in smaller schools. The quality of group relationships would be enhanced; problems with school order and discipline would be greatly diminished; and students and teachers would be more attached to each other and more identified with their schools.

Teachers and administrators can also modify the use of ability groups within classrooms so that heterogeneous groups become the norm. The literature suggests that this would help maintain academic norms within the classroom, enhance relationships among students within different ability levels, and raise teachers' academic expectations. At least two methods have demonstrated success in this area. One is the so-called Joplin method of grouping, where students attend heterogeneous classrooms most of the day but are regrouped across grade levels for only one period, often math. The cross-grade grouping allows the maintenance of larger groups, thus enhancing teacher contact time, but also allows for ability matching for effective use of resources. Because the grouping occurs for only one period during the day, most of students' time is spent in a heterogeneous setting, where there is a larger probability that more achievement-oriented norms will be enhanced.

The other widely accepted method of grouping to counter the use of ability groups is cooperative learning, where students work in small, cross-ability-level groups on assigned tasks (see Slavin 1990c). This technique seems to foster both instrumental and expressive goal attainment. Students achieve as well or better than they do in traditional settings, they are more motivated to learn, and they have higher self-esteem and better relationships with each other. These results hold across age groups, subject areas, and a wide range of tasks (Bossert 1988a; Wilkinson 1988).

If teachers retain ability groups, Maureen Hallinan (1987) suggests that they could alter their procedures to "provide greater equality of opportunities to learn for all students." This could be done through such methods as increasing the time spent with low-ability students, developing more challenging and engaging methods for lower groups, adjusting expectations for pupils when new information is available, being more flexible in moving students from one group to another, and modifying the reward structures so that membership in a lower group does not automatically result in negative reactions from peers (Hallinan 1987, pp. 65-66).

## THE ISSUE OF MIXED-SEX SCHOOLS

The striking exception to the evidence regarding heterogeneous learning groups involves the issue of mixed-sex secondary schooling. The literature reviewed in Chapter 1 suggests that single-sex schools enhance achievement, aspirations, attitudes toward learning, and positive views toward women's roles for girls from all racial and ethnic backgrounds and for Hispanic and African American boys. Anglo boys, in contrast, tend to do better on these dimensions when enrolled in mixed-sex schools. It is suggested that, for girls, the single-sex school allows an academic climate to predominate over the peer culture. For boys, the single-sex school still has a strong peer culture but is accompanied by a strong disciplinary climate, which accounts for the higher achievement of minority boys.

Liberal feminists have long advocated the end of single-sex schooling, assuming that it would doom girls to a second-class education. (See Stockard and Johnson 1992 for a discussion of this tradition.) If, however, girls' schools can have resources equivalent to those others receive, these results indicate that girls can best blossom academically when the constraints and pressures of a mixed-sex peer culture are minimized. Cornelius Riordan (1990, pp. 150-53) suggests that single-sex schools should be offered as an option for students and parents, noting that they would be just as, if not more, effective and less expensive to establish than many other proposed reforms, such as lengthening the school day or establishing magnet schools. If districts were to establish much smaller schools in an attempt to diminish tracking and magnet schools to promote desegregation, they could just as easily include single-sex schools as one of the options.

More than the other policy suggestions we have made, this proposal might be seen as having a trade-off, for Anglo boys do not appear to benefit from schooling in single-sex schools. Of special interest to feminists may be the fact that these boys actually have more tolerant attitudes toward women in mixed-sex schools than in single-sex schools. A great deal of evidence suggests that egalitarian relationships between the sex groups, such as those that occur under the guidance of adults, including teachers and parents, can mitigate the most sexually oppressive aspects of the male peer group (see Stockard and Johnson 1992). To the extent that girls would opt for single-sex schools, more boys would have to attend schools with fewer girl peers. These would probably still be coeducational, however, because it is unlikely that all girls would opt for single-sex schools.

## NEEDED RESEARCH

Although the research seems clear that heterogeneous groups generally promote greater learning, more academically oriented norms, and better use of teacher resources, relatively little research appears to have focused on the level of the child. This is especially true in the area of cooperative learning, where it is known that this process enhances achievement of all the children involved, but it is not clear how this occurs (see Bossert 1988a). One very productive research avenue could involve an exploration of this process. We suspect that such a research agenda would involve a merger of the "process-product" orientation toward research, which focuses on teacher behaviors, and the "input-output" orientation, which tends to focus on resources.

More research is also needed on the way in which single-sex learning environments affect student learning. The studies that are available come from the "input-output" tradition and provide no information on the processes involved in the learning situation. In addition, given the long tradition of coeducation in this country, there are only a very few single-sex schools that can be studied, and virtually all of these are affiliated with religious groups. Using a broader sample with data from countries other than the United States and different research methods could help provide better information on how the single-sex environment promotes learning and on the differential effects of this environment on different subgroups of students. As noted above, if single-sex schools were to become a viable option, it is unlikely that all girls would choose them, implying that a coeducational environment would still be available for boys. Yet this coeducational school would have a more imbalanced sex ratio than is currently found in most schools. The way in which such an imbalanced sex ratio would affect boys' attitudes could be addressed by further research. (See Guttentag and Secord 1983 for an extensive discussion of the way sex ratios within a society may influence behaviors.)

## Facilities and School and Classroom Size

Although a number of studies reviewed in Chapter 3 suggest that the nature of a school's facilities has little to do with student achievement, we contend that these results occurred because of methodological shortcomings with the studies. A closer examination of the data indicates that resources can directly affect children's learning, especially in the way that resources are allocated and directed toward individual children. When resources are broadly conceived of as time, materials, and pace of instruction (see Bidwell and Kasarda 1980; Barr and Dreeben 1983, 1985), it becomes clear that students who receive more of these resources also have higher achievement. Similarly, although some studies indicate that the size of a school or classroom does not affect students' learning, more carefully designed studies confirm the intuitive notion that student achievement is enhanced in smaller classrooms and smaller schools.

We believe that the policy implications of these results are clear. As a society, we cannot skimp on educational resources and expect our schools to be effective. Teachers and students deserve adequate resources, and they deserve to have these equitably distributed. State laws regarding certification maintain relatively similar curricular materials in all schools, and differences in access often reflect decisions of district- and school-level personnel regarding the allocation of these materials to students. Decisions regarding the time allocated to learning and the pace of instruction can vary a great deal across classrooms, schools, and districts (see Barr and Dreeben 1983), and these decisions can have a direct impact on children's learning. The evidence is clear that students who spend more time engaged in active learning and who move through the curriculum at an appropriate pace learn more (Carroll 1963; Barr and Dreeben 1983). Administrators and teachers can directly enhance students' learning environments by their decisions regarding time allocations and the pace of learning.

Teachers can more effectively devote time to students if they have smaller classes. Properly designed studies confirm the intuitive notion that students learn more in smaller classes. They also have more positive attitudes toward school and toward each other as well as higher achievement, once individual-level variables are controlled, in smaller schools. Group relations are more orderly, and relationships between teachers, administrators, and parents are better in small schools. In general, smaller schools and classrooms are much more conducive than larger groups to the development of social capital, a sense of community, and positive expressive and instrumental norms.

Although instituting smaller classes would require a substantial infusion of funds into the nation's schools, developing smaller schools could be much less costly. Because smaller schools are more orderly, fewer administrators would be required to deal with disciplinary problems, and the actual staff required would probably not increase much, if at all. At least initially, the current school buildings could be used, through such formats as the "school within a school" and magnet programs. As new schools are built, they could be designed to accommodate smaller student bodies. Heterogeneity of schools could be retained through the careful construction of magnet programs that would attract a wide variety of students. The departmentalization of high schools is well institutionalized, and smaller schools generally involve much weaker departments. Although teachers might feel wary about the weakening of departments and unsure about their ability to deal with a wider variety of responsibilities, the increased sense of control and collegiality that can develop in smaller schools could eventually offset these concerns. (See Gregory and Smith 1987 for an extended discussion of how smaller schools could be developed; also see Newmann 1981.)

Research on the relationship of student achievement to facilities and size no doubt will continue. Many of these analyses seem to have been politically motivated in the past, to try to justify certain expenditure levels. We can only hope that the problems in earlier research will become less common and that researchers will focus less on aggregated measures of resources and much more on how these resources are actually allocated by individual administrators and teachers and used by individual students. Similarly, research on the relationship of size to achievement needs to deal with a broad enough range of classrooms and school sizes to see the extent of possible relationships and examine the full way in which variations in size affect social actions and the establishment of effective social orders in schools.

## Effective Climates and Community Relations

In Chapter 2, we reviewed an extensive body of literature regarding school and classroom climates, that is, how the norms and relationships within educational groups affect student learning. This discussion indicated that student learning is enhanced in settings with high academic expectations, effective leadership, an orderly atmosphere, and warmth, concern, and respect for others. In the terms of our conceptual framework, school and classroom effectiveness is enhanced where strong instrumental and expressive norms are present within the social order and where they are infused in social actions. In Chapter 4, we examined the literature on the relationship between communities and schools. This discussion indicates that student learning is enhanced when parents are involved in children's schooling and when the relationships between parents, community members, and school officials are respectful, collaborative, and mutually supportive. All of the policy recommendations discussed above regarding student groups and resource allocations would enhance school and classroom climate. Additional policies that more directly deal with school and classroom climate and focus on students, teachers, communities, and parents are also important. In each of these policy areas, the importance of effective school leadership that involves concerns with both expressive and instrumental norms is apparent.

## ENHANCING STUDENT COMMITMENT

School officials, both teachers and administrators, can directly enhance each of the elements of school effectiveness. They can help establish high academic standards, an orderly environment, and warm, caring, respectful relationships within the school. Coleman and Hoffer (1987) directly address the way in which school principals can enhance school climates and the social capital that is available to students, recognizing that the relationships between students—the peer culture—are an exceedingly powerful influence on young people. They thus suggest "two goals for the principal: to have a student body sufficiently integrated and cohesive that it constitutes social capital which can be a force in the lives of students; and to direct that force toward, rather than away from, education" (Coleman and Hoffer 1987, p. 237).

This requires a principal that, in the terms of R. F. Bales, is both an "expressive leader," concerned with enhancing and maintaining interpersonal relationships within a group, and an "instrumental leader," concerned with maintaining and actively working toward goals of effective education. Although Bales's original research (1950) indicates that some group leaders specialize in either instrumental or expressive tasks, others incorporate both concerns within their leadership styles. It is these unique and especially skilled individuals who appear to be most effective as school administrators.

To promote the integration or social capital of the student body, Coleman and Hoffer suggest that schools have "collective events" in which all members can be involved. Competitions between other schools are suggested as one good way of doing this because they replace the interpersonal competition of the classroom with a common goal and accompanying social cohesion. The greater social bonds between students help to establish common social norms and create a natural community, an important step in developing an orderly, supportive school environment. The goal of the administrator is not just to develop such activities but also to work to ensure that all members of the community can participate in and enjoy them. This, as we have seen, is much easier to ensure within smaller schools.

Although some schools, especially those within small towns or cohesive neighborhoods, may already have student bodies with rich social capital, Coleman and Hoffer note that principals in all schools need to direct the social capital, or peer culture, of the students in directions that reinforce educational goals. Although the interschool competitions mentioned above often involve sports events, principals can actively work to encourage and honor academic accomplishments equally as often as athletic ones through the ways in which awards are distributed and the use of collective events in areas such as music, drama, debate, and mathematics (Coleman and Hoffer 1987, pp. 237-38). Here the goal of the administrator involves directing student activities and norms toward those that promote educational achievement and academic involvement rather than less academic goals often common within peer groups.

## ENHANCING TEACHER COMMITMENT

Brian Rowan (1990) notes that in the 1980s two different types of organizational reforms were proposed for schools. One, which he terms *control strategies,* tried to tighten the loose coupling of schools and increase bureaucratic controls over teaching and curriculum. This approach is based on the assumption that within loosely coupled schools educational goals are vague and that more explicit control over teaching methods and curriculum could counter this basic aspect of schools. The second method, commitment strategies, eschews bureaucratic controls as a way of improving schools and instead focuses on ways to develop working arrangements that support teachers' decision making and enhance their engagement and commitment to teaching and their schools. This approach recognizes that teaching is as much art as it is science, that it involves many complex and nonroutine tasks that cannot be adequately programmed from moment to moment if students' needs are to be adequately met. Supporters of this approach advocate collaborative and participative school management techniques, where teachers are intimately involved and responsible for decisions regarding curriculum, time allocation, and other areas directly related to teaching.

These models have rarely been fully applied. Yet the literature we reviewed in Chapter 2 suggests that teachers are more satisfied with their work and more motivated in schools where they have more opportunities for collegial interchanges and where they can help define and develop school policies and goals. Just as greater bureaucratic controls can counter the loose coupling of schools, Susan Rosenholtz (1989; see also Rosenholtz and Simpson 1990) notes that greater joint involvement in classrooms can counter the isolation many teachers experience as a result of schools' loosely coupled organization. Through developing school structures that encourage teachers to work together, the inherent difficulty of teaching can be made an overt issue, and ways to develop more effective teaching methods can become a day-to-day part of school life. As teachers continually learn more about teaching, both from their colleagues and from outside experts, they develop a sense of mastery and greater control over their environment. In addition, with more autonomy and discretion regarding their teaching tasks, they feel more empowered, realizing that their students' success is a direct function of their own instructional efforts. The psychic rewards that come from this sense of accomplishment help build greater commitment to the school and to the students, thus enhancing a more effective climate. Rosenholtz has found that teachers who feel competent and valued are very likely to try even harder to improve their performance (see Rosenholtz 1989).

Developing such a collaborative and committed work environment requires skilled principals, ones who can be both expressive leaders and instrumental leaders. They must be attuned to the relationships among teachers and how these may best be supported and developed; they must also be able to provide the best technical support possible for developing better instructional strategies. In addition, they must be flexible and prepared to provide different types of support for teachers at different stages of their careers and with different types of needs (Rosenholtz and Simpson 1990).

In addition to good leadership, teachers need time. It is doubtful, given the very extensive time demands most teachers face on a day-to-day basis, if many would have time left over for extensive involvement in curricular planning and other management issues without alterations in their schedules. Time is one of the most crucial resources in schools. Providing more of this crucial resource to teachers through alterations in staffing patterns and other innovations seems essential if any real involvement of teachers in governance is to occur (see Flinders 1989).

## ENHANCING PARENTAL AND COMMUNITY INVOLVEMENT

The third crucial element of effective schools is parents and community members, and many reviews note the importance of parental involvement in children's achievement and the importance of community support in developing effective schools. In summarizing his research based on a large number of schools in different communities, John Goodlad (1984, p. 272) asserted that "our schools will get better and have continuing good health only to the degree that a significant proportion of our people, not just parents, care about them." Many experts believe that the appropriate place to promote greater parental and community involvement is at the school rather than the district level (e.g., Goodlad 1984, 1987; Joyce et al. 1983). People can more easily identify with and work with individual schools than with a conglomeration of many units. The issue then becomes how best to promote this involvement and to help it develop in a way that enhances schools as supportive communities and as effective learning environments.

Bastian and associates (1986) discuss two specific methods of establishing community-school links: youth advocacy programs and the use of paraprofessionals in the schools. Youth advocacy programs are designed by a committee of interested parents who formulate and disseminate school policy suggestions that represent the needs of parents and students. These parental committees can also be actively involved in distributing information about school policies, performance, and programs to the wider community of parents, seeking their opinions and suggestions about current school governance. Local residents can also serve as paraprofessionals by volunteering as tutors, teacher aides, and special program instructors. These strategies are designed to promote healthy relations between schools and communities, but they also help enhance a school's learning environment. They promote more orderly schools, reduce teacher/student ratios, promote small groups with instrumental norms, and allow parents to be directly involved with their children's educational experiences.

Coleman and Hoffer (1987) suggest that school principals should actively try to promote social capital among parents by developing opportunities for them to strengthen their relations with each other and with the school. Through parents' meetings and encouraging parental participation in school events, principals can promote more extensive and intensive relationships among the members of the school community, which is the social capital available to students. Coleman and Hoffer see this social capital as an extremely important resource in individual students' achievement.

In addition, school administrators can develop strategies for greater involvement of parents and community members in the governance and improvement of individual schools. Bruce Joyce, Richard Hersh, and Michael McKibbin have proposed such a strategy of school improvement. Recognizing that schools, like all organizations, are resistant to change, they propose a process that would build continual evaluation and processes of improvement into the regular organizational life of individual schools. This process involves an organization, called the Responsible Parties, composed of representatives of the general public, site administrators and representatives of the larger school district administration, teachers, technical consultants, and patrons of the school (parents and, when appropriate, children). This committee would be responsible for openly building, supporting, evaluating, and rethinking the school's program. By involving representatives of all parties interested in a school's program, this process can help ensure that the program is intelligible to all the parties; that conflicts over alternatives can be recognized and either resolved or dealt with in a mutually acceptable manner; that debate over the program is open and reasonable, thus helping to develop support for the school; and that coordination occurs among administrators, teachers, and community members (see Joyce et al. 1983, pp. 86-87).

This process implicitly takes into account each of the elements of our conceptual framework presented in Chapter 5. It recognizes the importance of both expressive and instrumental norms within the social order. It also recognizes the importance of group relationships or social action in legitimizing these norms and that conflict and differences will be a regular part of any type of decision-making activity or social action. It recognizes that all members of a school community have a legitimate voice in shaping the nature of the school and, in turn, helps alleviate the barriers to participation noted in Chapter 4. It also proposes a strategy by which all parties can have input and where a solution can be developed that all can accept.

Again, developing collaborative governance models such as that envisioned by Joyce and his associates requires the work of skilled and dedicated administrators. They need to be both expressive and instrumental leaders: attuned to the interpersonal needs of a group while also directing attention to goals of higher achievement. Special care will need to be taken in heterogeneous communities to ensure that representatives of all parts of the community are included, feel that they are a part of the school community, and can come to engage in fruitful relationships with teachers and administrators and other parents.

## NEEDED RESEARCH

More research is needed to determine how good school-community relationships develop and to explore how positive relationships can be enhanced in a wide variety of community settings. More research is also needed to examine how community values influence school climates and how this influence may vary from one type of community to another and between schools with varying student compositions. It is possible that closer ties between communities and schools may promote the development of positive expressive norms within schools and better interpersonal relationships among school members. At the same time, prevailing community values may work against the establishment of instrumental norms promoting optimum achievement, perhaps through the promotion of traditional community practices and insularity. To what extent do these two processes affect each other? How may both positive expressive and positive instrumental norms be enhanced with the optimum development of positive noncognitive traits and academic achievement?

It is also important to examine how the various aspects of students' environments are associated with each other. More definitive studies of the relationships between community type and attitudes, school facilities (including teachers' characteristics) and organization, school climate, and groupings of students are needed. Studies are also needed that take into account how variations in students' demographic characteristics, such as their gender, ability, socioeconomic status, and race and ethnicity, affect their relationships with others within a school and their attachment to school norms. It is conceivable that characteristics of teachers and administrators would also affect the relationship between students' characteristics and their attachment to school norms, and this relationship needs to be investigated too.

## Summary

Our overview of policies that could help produce more effective educational environments has been based on our review of the empirical literature in Chapters 1 to 4 and our discussion of theories dealing with environmental influences in Chapter 5. In Chapter 5, we suggested that the wide range of literature regarding environmental influences could be summarized within a parsimonious framework that sees effective learning environments as reflecting both the *social order*—the norms and values within a group—and *social action*—the relationships between members of the group and their interactions and choices. We have stressed that both expressive and instrumental orientations are crucial to the development of effective social orders and social actions in schools and classrooms. Effective educational environments exhibit high achievement expectations and a large proportion of task-related activities within emotionally supportive and accepting atmospheres. Given the heterogeneous nature of many schools and communities, it will not always be easy to develop such supportive environments and agreed-upon goals. Resistance and disagreement over school policies may be an inevitable part of the process of developing social orders that are acceptable to and legitimated by all members of a school's community.

The policy recommendations above reflect our relatively simple conceptual framework. We suggest that more effective schools would be heterogeneous in nature and use heterogeneous learning groups as much as possible. These schools should be relatively small in size and have, whenever possible, small classrooms. Administrators should be both skilled expressive and skilled instrumental leaders. They should try to develop school climates that can increase students' commitment to each other as a group and enhance academically related norms and values. They should also try to develop work environments that can involve teachers in collaborative decision making and develop school governance structures that incorporate representatives of parents and the community. It must be recognized that this school governance structure will probably involve conflict over orientations and goals. Procedures will need to be developed that can accommodate differing perspectives and allow movement toward mutually acceptable solutions within a respectful and accepting environment.

None of our recommendations is specific in nature and our conceptual framework is purposely broad in scope. Many of the authors cited here have much more detailed recommendations and conceptual models. As we noted in Chapter 4, communities vary a great deal, and specific procedures that might produce effective schools in one community would not be as effective in another (see McLaughlin and Talbert 1990). Governing bodies that represent responsible parties for a particular school can probably judge best what types of changes would be most helpful for that school. Because our framework and recommendations are general, rather than specific, we believe that they can be applied and adapted to a variety of settings. We believe that the changes we have proposed can be incorporated in both public and private systems, in large cities, in suburbs, and in rural communities. With the exception of the recommendation for smaller classrooms, none of the proposed changes would be exorbitantly expensive, although all would require at least some additional costs in either time or money. We believe, however, that these costs would be well worth it. The future of any society depends upon the health and well-being of its children.

Inherent in our conceptual framework is the notion that social actions—the choices and decisions of individuals—directly determine the social order—the characteristics of schools. Many policymakers, teachers, administrators, and parents want to develop more effective educational environments. They have the energy and the desire to alter schools and classrooms. The research and theoretical literature presented in this book suggest that educational environments can affect children's learning. By using these insights, people concerned with quality education can create more effective environments in their own communities.

## Note

1. James Coleman and others (e.g., Coleman 1977, 1987a, 1987c; ASCD Panel 1990) have suggested that techniques of allowing parents to choose the school their children will attend through some type of voucherlike system could be the most effective, efficient, and humane means to promote greater attachment of parents and children to schools as well as racial and ethnic desegregation. These proposals essentially extend the magnet school concept to the entire range of both public and private schools. The issues raised by these authors go far beyond what can be discussed in this volume. Suffice it to say that our analysis of and proposals for effective educational environments apply to both private and public schools.

# References


Aikins, M. 1968. *Economy of Scale in the Production of Selected Educational Outcomes.* Washington, DC: AERA.

Alexander, J. C. 1982a. *Theoretical Logic in Sociology. Vol. 1, Positivism, Presuppositions, and Current Controversies.* Berkeley: University of California Press.

———. 1982b. *Theoretical Logic in Sociology. Vol. 2, The Antimonies of Classical Thought: Marx and Durkheim.* Berkeley: University of California Press.

———. 1983a. *Theoretical Logic in Sociology. Vol. 3. The Classical Attempt at Theoretical Synthesis: Max Weber.* Berkeley: University of California Press.

———. 1983b. *Theoretical Logic in Sociology. Vol. 4. The Modern Reconstruction of Classical Thought: Talcott Parsons.* Berkeley: University of California Press.

———. 1984. "Social-Structural Analysis: Some Notes on Its History and Prospects." *The Sociological Quarterly* 25:5-26.

———. 1985. "Introduction." Pp. 7-18 in *Neofunctionalism,* edited by J. C. Alexander. Beverly Hills, CA: Sage.

———. 1987. "Action and Its Environments." In *The Micro-Macro Link,* edited by J. C. Alexander, B. Giesen, R. Munch, and N. J. Smelser. Berkeley: University of California Press.

Alexander, J. C. and B. Giesen. 1987. "From Reduction to Linkage: The Long View of the Micro-Macro Debate." Pp. 1-42 in *The Micro-Macro Link,* edited by J. C. Alexander, B. Giesen, R. Munch, and N. J. Smelser. Berkeley: University of California Press.

Alexander, K. L. and M. A. Cook. 1982. "Curricula and Coursework: A Surprise Ending to a Familiar Story." *American Sociological Review* 47:626-40.

Alexander, K. L., M. A. Cook, and E. L. McDill. 1978. "Curriculum Tracking and Educational Stratification: Some Further Evidence." *American Sociological Review* 43:47-66.

Alexander, K. L. and B. K. Eckland. 1975. "Contextual Effects in the High School Attainment Process." *American Sociological Review* 40:402-16.

Alexander, K. L., D. Entwisle, and M. Thomson. 1987. "School Performance, Status Relations, and the Structure of Sentiment: Bringing the Teacher Back In." *American Sociological Review* 52:665-82.

Alexander, K. L. and E. L. McDill. 1976. "Selection and Allocation Within Schools: Some Causes and Consequences of Curriculum Placement." *American Sociological Review* 41:963-80.

Alexander, K. L., E. McDill, J. Fennessey, and R. D'Amico. 1979. "School SES Influences: Composition or Context?" *Sociology of Education* 52:222-37.

Alexander, K. L., G. Natriello, and A. Pallas. 1985. "For Whom the School Bell Tolls: The Impact of Dropping Out on Cognitive Performance." *American Sociological Review* 50: 409-20.

Altman, E. R. 1959. "The Effect of Rank in Class and Size of High School on the Academic Achievement of Central Michigan College Seniors Class of 1957." *Journal of Educational Research* 52:307-9.

Alwin, D. F. and L. B. Otto. 1977. "High School Context Effects on Aspirations." *Sociology of Education* 50:259-73.

Anderson, C. S. 1982. "The Search for School Climate: A Review of the Research." *Review of Educational Research* 52:368-420.

Anderson, G. J. 1970. "Effects of Classroom Social Climate on Individual Learning." *American Education Research Journal* 7(2):135-52.

Anderson, G. J. and H. J. Walberg. 1968. "Classroom Climate and Group Learning" *International Journal of Educational Sciences* 2:175-80.

———. 1972. "Class Size and the Social Environment of Learning: A Mixed Replication and Extension." *Alberta Journal of Educational Research* 18:277-86.

Apple, M. W. 1982. *Education and Power.* Boston: Routledge & Kegan Paul.

———. 1988. *Teachers and Texts.* New York: Routledge & Kegan Paul.

Armor, D., P. Conry-Oseguera, M. Cox, N. King, L. McDonnell, A. Pascal, E. Paul, and G. Zellman. 1976. *Analysis of the School Preferred Reading Program in Selected Los Angeles Minority Schools* (Report No. R-2007-LAUSD). Santa Monica, CA: Rand Corporation.

Armor, D. J. 1972. "The Evidence on Busing." *The Public Interest* 28:90-126.

ASCD Panel. 1990. *Public Schools of Choice.* Alexandria, VA: Association for Supervision and Curriculum Development.

Ashton, P. T. and R. B. Webb. 1986. *Making a Difference: Teachers' Sense of Efficacy and Student Achievement.* New York: Longman.

Austin, G. R. 1979. "Exemplary Schools and the Search for Effectiveness." *Educational Leadership* 37:10-14.

Averch, H. A., S. J. Carroll, T. S. Donaldson, H. J. Kiesling, and J. Pincus. 1974. *How Effective Is Schooling? A Critical Review of Research.* Englewood Cliffs, NJ: Educational Technology.

Baas, A. M. 1973. "Community Schools." *Educational Management Review* 24. Clearinghouse on Educational Management, University of Oregon, Eugene.

Bachman, J. G. and P. M. O'Malley. 1986. "Self-Concepts, Self-Esteem, and Education Experiences: The Frog-Pond Revisited (Again)." *Journal of Personality and Social Psychology* 50: 35-46.

Bain, R. K. and J. G. Anderson. 1974. "School Context and Peer Influences on Educational Plans of Adolescents." *Review of Educational Research* 44:429-45.

Baird, L. 1969. "Big School, Small School: A Critical Examination of the Hypothesis." *Journal of Educational Psychology* 60:253-60.

Bales, R. F. 1950. *Interaction Process Analysis: A Method for the Study of Small Groups.* Cambridge, MA: Addison-Wesley.

Ball, S. J. 1981. *Beachside Comprehensive: A Case-Study of Secondary Schooling.* Cambridge, UK: Cambridge University Press.

Barker, R. G. 1968. *Ecological Psychology: Concepts and Methods for Studying the Environment of Human Behavior.* Stanford, CA: Stanford University Press.

———. 1978. "Return Trip, 1977." Pp. 285-96 in *Habitats, Environments, and Human Behavior,* by R. G. Barker and associates. San Francisco: Jossey-Bass.

Barker, R. G. and P. V. Gump. 1964. *Big School, Small School.* Stanford, CA: Stanford University Press.

Barker, R. G. and associates. 1978. *Habitats, Environments, and Human Behavior.* San Francisco: Jossey-Bass.

Barr, R. and R. Dreeben, with N. Wiratchai. 1983. *How Schools Work.* Chicago: University of Chicago Press.

Barr, R. and R. Dreeben. 1985. "A Sociological Perspective on School Time." Pp. 109-17 in *Perspectives on Instructional Time,* edited by C. W. Fisher and D. C. Berliner. New York: Longman.

Barraclough, T. 1973. "Community Control of Schools." *Educational Management Review* 26. Clearinghouse on Educational Management, University of Oregon, Eugene.

Bastian, A., N. Fruchter, M. Gittel, C. Greer, and K. Haskins. 1986. *Choosing Equality: The Case for Democratic Schooling.* Philadelphia: Temple University Press.

Bauch, J. P. 1990. "The TransParent School: A Partnership for Parent Involvement." *Educational Horizons* 68:187-89.

Bauch, P. A. 1988. "Is Parent Involvement Different in Private Schools?" *Educational Horizons* 66:78-82.

Beckerman, T. M. and T. L. Good. 1981. "The Classroom Ratio of High- and Low-Aptitude Students and Its Effect on Achievement." *American Educational Research Journal* 18:317-27.

Begle, E. G. 1975. *Ability Grouping for Mathematics Instruction: A Review of the Empirical Literature.* Stanford, CA: Stanford University, Mathematics Education Study Group. (ERIC Document Reproduction Service No. ED 116 938)

Berliner, D. 1979. "Tempus Educare." In *Research on Teaching: Concepts, Findings, and Implications,* edited by P. Peterson and H. Walberg. Berkeley, CA: McCutchan.

Bidwell, C. E. 1965. "The School as a Formal Organization." In *Handbook of Organization,* edited by J. G. March. Chicago: Rand McNally.

Bidwell, C. E. and J. D. Kasarda. 1975. "School District Organization and Student Achievement." *American Sociological Review* 40:55-70.

Bidwell, C. E. and J. D. Kasarda. 1980. "Conceptualizing and Measuring the Effects of School and Schooling." *American Journal of Education* 88:401-30.

Blau, P. M. 1960. "Structural Effects." *American Sociological Review* 25:178-93.

———. 1977. *Inequality and Heterogeneity: A Primitive Theory of Social Structure.* New York: Free Press.

Blau, P. M. and O. D. Duncan. 1967. *The American Occupational Structure.* New York: John Wiley.

Blau, P. M. and J. E. Schwartz. 1984. *Crosscutting Social Circles: Testing a Macrostructural Theory of Intergroup Relations.* Orlando, FL: Academic Press.

Blumer, H. 1969. *Symbolic Interactionism.* Englewood Cliffs, NJ: Prentice-Hall.

Boocock, S. S. 1966. "Toward a Sociology of Learning: A Selective Review of Existing Research." *Sociology of Education* 39:867-79.

Bossert, S. T. 1988a. "Cooperative Activities in the Classroom." *Review of Research in Education* 15:225-50.

———. 1988b. "School Effects." Pp. 341-52 in *Handbook of Research on Educational Administration,* edited by N. J. Boyan. New York: Longman.

Bossert, S. T. et al. 1982. "The Instructional Management Role of the Principal." *Educational Administration Quarterly* 8:34-36.

Bourgeois, A. D. 1969. "Community Control and Urban Conflict." *Theory into Practice* 8:243-46.

Bowles, S. and H. Gintis. 1976. *Schooling in Capitalist America.* New York: Basic Books.

Bowles, S. S. 1969. *Educational Production Function: Final Report.* Washington, DC: U.S. Department of Health, Education and Welfare, Office of Education.

Boyer, E. L. 1983. *High School: A Report on Secondary Education in America.* New York: Harper & Row.

Boyle, R. P. 1966. "The Effect of High School on Students' Aspirations." *American Journal of Sociology* 71:628-39.

Braddock, J. H., II, R. L. Crain, and J. M. McPartland. 1984. "A Long-Term View of School Desegregation: Some Recent Studies of Graduates as Adults." *Phi Delta Kappan* 66:259-64.

Braddock, J. H., II and M. P. Dawkins. 1984. "Long-Term Effects of School Desegregation on Southern Blacks." *Sociological Spectrum* 4: 365-81.

Bradley, L. and G. Bradley. 1977. "The Academic Achievement of Black Students in Desegregated Schools." *Review of Educational Research* 47:399-449.

Breckenridge, E. 1976. "Improving School Climate." *Phi Delta Kappan* 59:314-18.

Bridge, R. G., C. M. Judd, and P. R. Moock. 1979. *The Determinants of Educational Outcomes: The Impact of Families, Peers, Teachers, and Schools.* Cambridge, MA: Ballinger.

Brimer, A., G. F. Madaus, B. Chapman, T. Kellaghan, and R. Wood. 1978. *Sources of Difference in School Achievement.* London: National Foundation for Educational Research.

Brookover, W. B., C. Beady, P. Flood, J. Schweitzer, and J. Wisenbaker. 1979. *School Social Systems and Student Achievement.* New York: Praeger.

Brookover, W. B. and L. W. Lezotte. 1979. *Changes in School Characteristics Coincident With Changes in Student Achievement.* Washington, DC: National Institute of Education. (ERIC Document Reproduction Service No. ED 181 005)

Brookover W. B. and J. M. Schneider. 1975. "Academic Environments and Elementary School Achievement." *Journal of Research and Development in Education* 9:82-91.

Brookover, W. B., J. H. Schweitzer, J. M. Schneider, C. H. Beady, P. K. Flood, and J. M. Wisenbaker. 1978. "Elementary School Social Climate and School Achievement." *American Educational Research Journal* 15:301-18.

Brophy, J. E. 1979. "Teacher Behavior and Its Effects." *Journal of Educational Psychology* 71:733-50.

———. 1986. "Teacher Influences on Student Achievement." *American Psychologist* 41:1069-77.

Brophy, J. E. and C. Evertson. 1976. *Learning From Teaching: A Developmental Perspective.* Boston: Allyn & Bacon.

Brophy, J. E. and T. L. Good. 1986. "Teacher Behavior and Student Achievement." In *Handbook of Research on Teaching*, edited by M. C. Wittrock. New York: Macmillan.

Brown, B. W. and D. H. Saks. 1980. "Production Technologies and Resource Allocations Within Classrooms and Schools: Theory and Measurement." In *The Analysis of Educational Productivity. Vol. 1, Issues in Microanalysis*, edited by R. Dreeben and J. A. Thomas. Cambridge, MA: Ballinger.

Cahen, L. S., N. Filby, G. McCutcheon, and D. W. Kyle. 1983. *Class Size and Instruction.* New York: Longman.

Callahan, R. E. 1962. *Education and the Cult of Efficiency: A Study of the Social Forces That Have Shaped the Administration of the Public Schools.* Chicago: University of Chicago Press.

Campbell, E. Q. and C. N. Alexander. 1965. "Structural Effects and Interpersonal Relationships." *American Journal of Sociology* 71:284-9.

Campbell, J., M. D. Dunnette, E. E. Lawler, and K. E. Weick. 1970. *Managerial Behavior, Performance, and Effectiveness.* New York: McGraw-Hill.

Campbell, W. J. 1964. "Some Effects of High School Consolidation." In *Big School, Small School*, edited by R. G. Barker and P. V. Gump. Stanford, CA: Stanford University Press.

Carroll, J. B. 1963. "A Model of School Learning." *Teachers College Record* 64:723-33.

Centra, J. A. and D. A. Potter. 1980. "School and Teacher Effects: An Interrelational Model." *Review of Educational Research* 50:273-91.

Cervone, B. T. and K. O'Leary. 1982. "A Conceptual Framework for Parent Involvement." *Educational Leadership* 40:48-9.

Chavkin, N. F. 1990. "Joining Forces: Education for a Changing Population." *Educational Horizons* 68:190-96.

Childs, T. S. and C. Shakeshaft. 1986. "A Meta-Analysis of Research on the Relationship Between Educational Expenditures and Student Achievement." *Journal of Education Finance* 12:249-63.

Christenson, J. A. 1984. "Gemeinschaft and Gesellschaft: Testing the Spatial and Communal Hypotheses." *Social Forces* 62:160-68.

Chubb, J. E. 1988. "Why the Current Wave of School Reform Will Fail." *The Public Interest* 86:28-49.

Clements, W. H. 1970. *Ideal High School Size: A Mirage in the Desert.* Stevens Point: Wisconsin State University. (ERIC Document Reproduction Service No. ED 055 689)

Cohen, D. K. 1969. "The Price of Community Control." *Theory into Practice* 8:231-341.

Cohen, E. G., R. A. Flotan, and C. Leechor. 1989. "Can Classrooms Learn?" *Sociology of Education* 62:75-94.

Cohen, M. 1983. "Instructional Management and Social Conditions in Effective Schools." In *School Finance and School Improvement: Linkages in the 1980s*, edited by A. O. Webb and L. D. Webb. Cambridge, MA: Ballinger.

Cohn, E. and S. D. Millman. 1975. *Input-Output Analysis in Public Education.* Cambridge, MA: Ballinger.

Coleman, J. S. 1977. "Introduction: Choice in American Education." In *Parents, Teachers, and Children: Prospects for Choice in American Education*, edited by J. S. Coleman et al. San Francisco: Institute for Contemporary Studies.

———. 1982. "Public Schools, Private Schools, and the Public Interest." *American Education* 18:17-22.

———. 1986a. *Individual Interests and Collective Action: Studies in Rationality and Social Change.* Cambridge: Cambridge University Press.

———. 1986b. "Social Theory, Social Research, and a Theory of Action." *American Journal of Sociology* 91:1309-35.

———. 1987a. "Families and Schools." *Educational Researcher* 16:32-38.

———. 1987b. "Microfoundations and Macrosocial Behavior." Pp. 153-73 in *The Micro-Macro Link,* edited by J. C. Alexander, B. Giesen, R. Munch, and N. J. Smelser. Berkeley: University of California Press.

———. 1987c. "Relations Between School and Social Structure." Pp. 177-204 in *The Social Organization of Schools: New Conceptualizations of the Learning Process*, edited by M. T. Hallinan. New York: Plenum.

———. 1988. "Social Capital in the Creation of Human Capital." *American Journal of Sociology* 94:S95-S120.

———. 1990. *Foundations of Social Theory.* Cambridge, MA: Harvard University Press.

Coleman, J. S., E. Q. Campbell, C. F. Hobson, J. McPartland, A. M. Mood, F. D. Weinfeld, and R. L. York. 1966. *Equality of Educational Opportunity.* Washington, DC: U.S. Department of Health, Education and Welfare, Office of Education.

Coleman, J. S. and T. Hoffer. 1987. *Public and Private High Schools: The Impact of Communities.* New York: Basic Books.

Coleman, J. S., T. Hoffer, and S. Kilgore. 1982. *High School Achievement: Public, Catholic, and Private Schools Compared.* New York: Basic Books.

Collins, C. H., O. C. Moles, and M. Cross. 1982. *The Home-School Connection: Selected Partnership Programs in Large Cities.* Boston: Institute for Responsive Education.

Collins, R. 1979. *The Credential Society: An Historical Sociology of Education and Stratification.* New York: Academic Press.

Comer, J. P. 1980. *School Power: Implications of an Intervention Project.* New York: Free Press.

———. 1991. "Parent Participation: Fad or Function?" *Educational Horizons* 69:182-88.

Conant, J. B. 1959. *The American High School Today: A First Report to Interested Citizens.* New York: McGraw-Hill.

Cookson, P. W., Jr., and C. H. Persell. 1985. *Preparing for Power: America's Elite Boarding Schools.* New York: Basic Books.

Corcoran, T. B. 1990. "Schoolwork: Perspectives on Workplace Reform in Public Schools." Pp. 142-66 in *The Contexts of Teacher in Secondary Schools: Teachers' Realities,* edited by M. W. McLaughlin, J. E. Talbert, and N. Bascia. New York: Teachers College Press.

Crain, R. L. 1971. "School Integration and the Academic Achievement of Negroes." *Sociology of Education* 44:1-26.

Crain, R. L. and R. E. Mahard. 1983. "The Effect of Research Methodology on Desegregation-Achievement Studies: A Meta-Analysis." *American Journal of Sociology* 88:839-54.

Crane, J. 1991. "The Epidemic Theory of Ghettos and Neighborhood Effects on Dropping Out and Teenage Childbearing." *American Journal of Sociology* 96:1226-59.

Cremin, L. 1957. *The Republic and the School.* New York: Teachers College Press.

Cronbach, L. J. and R. E. Snow. 1977. *Aptitudes and Instructional Methods: A Handbook for Research on Interactions.* New York: Irvington.

Cusick, P. A. 1973. *Inside High School: The Student's World.* New York: Holt, Rinehart & Winston.

———. 1983. *The Egalitarian Ideal and the American High School.* New York: Longman.

Davies, D. 1981. "Citizen Participation in Decision Making in the Schools." Pp. 83-119 in *Communities and Their Schools,* edited by D. Davies. New York: McGraw-Hill.

Davis, C. 1970. "Approaches to Black Education." *Integrated Education* 8:45-50.

Davis, J. A. 1966. "The Campus as a Frog Pond: An Application of the Theory of Relative Deprivation to Career Decisions of College Men." *American Journal of Sociology* 72:17-31.

Davis, S. A. and E. J. Haller. 1981. "Tracking, Ability and SES: Further Evidence on the 'Revisionist-Meritocratic Debate.'" *American Journal of Education* 89:283-304.

Day, W. C. 1979. "Are Small Schools Better?" *School Business Affairs* 45:32-33.

Devereux, E. C., Jr. 1961. "Parsons' Sociological Theory." Pp. 1-63 in *The Social Theories of Talcott Parsons*, edited by M. Black. Englewood Cliffs, NJ: Prentice-Hall.

Dewar, J. 1964. "Grouping for Arithmetic Instruction in Sixth Grade." *Elementary School Journal* 63:266-69.

Dodendorf, D. M. 1983. "A Unique Rural School Environment." *Psychology in the Schools* 20:99-104.

Dornbusch, S. M. and P. L. Ritter. 1988. "Parents of High School Students: A Neglected Resource." *Educational Horizons* 66:75-77.

Downey, R. G. 1978. "Differences Between Entering Freshmen From Different Size High Schools." *Journal of College Student Personnel* 19:353-58.

Dreeben, R. 1968. *On What Is Learned in School.* Reading, MA: Addison-Wesley.

———. 1973. "The School as a Workplace." In *Second Handbook of Research on Teaching*, edited by R. Travers. Chicago: Rand McNally.

Dreeben, R. and R. Barr. 1987. "An Organizational Analysis of Curriculum and Instruction." Pp. 13-39 in *The Social Organization of Schools: New Conceptualizations of the Learning Process*, edited by M. T. Hallinan. New York: Plenum.

———. 1988. "Classroom Composition and the Design of Instruction." *Sociology of Education* 61:129-42.

Dreeben, R. and A. Gamoran. 1986. "Race, Instruction and Learning." *American Sociological Review* 51:660-69.

Duke, D. L. and C. Perry. 1978. "Can Alternative Schools Succeed Where Benjamin Spock, Spiro Agnew and B. F. Skinner Have Failed?" *Adolescence* 13:375-92.

Duncan, O. D., D. L. Featherman, and B. Duncan. 1972. *Socioeconomic Background and Achievement.* New York: Seminar.

Dunkin, M. and B. J. Biddle. 1974. *The Study of Teaching.* New York: Holt, Rinehart & Winston.

Dunne, F. 1977. "Choosing Smallness: An Examination of the Small School Experience in Rural America." Pp. 81-124 in *Education in Rural America: A Reassessment of Conventional Wisdom*, edited by J. P. Sher. Boulder, CO: Westview.

Durkheim, É. 1903/1961. *Moral Education.* New York: Free Press.

———. 1912/1915. *Elementary Forms of Religious Life.* New York: Free Press.

———. 1933. *The Division of Labor in Society*, translated by G. Simpson. New York: Macmillan.

Dwyer, D. C. 1984. "Forging Successful Schools: Realistic Expectations for Principals." *Educational Horizons* 63:3-8.

Eaton, W. E. 1990. "The Vulnerability of School Superintendents: The Thesis Reconsidered." In *Shaping the Superintendency: A Reexamination of Callahan and the Cult of Efficiency*. New York: Teachers College Press.

Eberle, N. 1983. "The Little School That Has It All." *Educational Horizons* 61:111-15.

Eberts, R. W., E. Kehoe, and J. A. Stone. 1983. *Determinants of Student Outcomes: The Roles of Collective Bargaining and School Size*. Eugene: University of Oregon, Center for Educational Policy and Management.

Eberts, R. W., E. K. Schwartz, and J. A. Stone. 1990. "School Reform, School Size, and Student Achievement." *Economic Review* 26(2):2-15.

Eckert, P. 1989. *Jocks and Burnouts: Social Categories and Identity in the High School*. New York: Teachers College Press.

Eder, D. 1983. "Ability Grouping and Students' Academic Self-Concepts: A Case Study." *Elementary School Journal* 84:149-61.

Edmonds, R. 1979a. "Effective Schools for the Urban Poor." *Educational Leadership* 37:15-24.

———. 1979b. "Some Schools Work and More Can." *Social Policy* 9:28-32.

Ellett, C. D. and H. J. Walberg. 1979. "Principals' Competency, Environment, and Outcomes." In *Educational Environments and Effects*, edited by H. J. Walberg. Berkeley, CA: McCutchan.

Entwisle, D. R. and L. A. Hayduk. 1982. *Early Schooling*. Baltimore: Johns Hopkins University Press.

Epstein, J. L. 1988. "How Do We Improve Programs for Parent Involvement?" *Educational Horizons* 66:58-59.

Epstein, J. L. and J. M. McPartland. 1976. "The Concept and Measurement of the Quality of School Life." *American Educational Research Journal* 13:15-30.

Esposito, D. 1973. "Homogeneous and Heterogeneous Ability Grouping: Principal Findings and Implications for Evaluating and Designing More Effective Education Environments." *Review of Educational Research* 43:163-79.

Everhart, R. B. 1983. "Classroom Management, Student Opposites, and the Job Process." In *Ideology and Practice in Schooling*, edited by M. W. Apple and L. Weis. Philadelphia: Temple University Press.

Eyler, J., V. J. Cook, and L. E. Ward. 1983. "Resegregation: Segregation Within Desegregated Schools." In *The Consequences of School De-*

*segregation*, edited by C. H. Rossell and W. D. Hawley. Philadelphia: Temple University Press.

Falk, W. W. and T. K. Pinhey. 1978. "Making Sense of the Concept Rural and Doing Rural Sociology: An Interpretative Perspective." *Rural Sociology* 43:547-58.

Fantini, M., M. Gittell, and R. Magat. 1970. *Community Control and the Urban School.* New York: Praeger.

Felmlee, D. and D. Eder. 1983. "Contextual Effects in the Classroom: The Impact of Ability Groups on Student Attention." *Sociology of Education* 56:77-87.

Felson, R. B. and M. D. Reed. 1986. "Reference Groups and Self-Appraisals of Academic Ability and Performance." *Social Psychology Quarterly* 49:103-9.

Field, R. H. and M. A. Abelson. 1982. "Climate: A Reconceptualization and Proposed Model." *Human Relations* 35:181-201.

Filby, N. N. and B. G. Barnett. 1982. "Student Perceptions of 'Better Readers' in Elementary Classrooms." *Elementary School Journal* 82:435-49.

Filby, N., B. Barnett, and S. Bossert. 1982. *Grouping Practices and Their Consequences.* San Francisco: Far West Laboratory for Educational Research.

Finley, M. K. 1984. "Teachers and Tracking in a Comprehensive High School." *Sociology of Education* 57:233-43.

Finn, C. E., Jr. 1991. *We Must Take Charge: Our Schools and Our Future.* New York: Free Press.

Finn, J. D. 1989. "Withdrawing From School." *Review of Educational Research* 59:117-42.

Firestone, W. A. and B. L. Wilson. 1983. *Using Bureaucratic and Cultural Linkages to Improve Instruction: The High School Principal's Contributions.* Philadelphia: Research for Better Schools.

Fisher, C. W. and D. C. Berliner, eds. 1985. *Perspectives on Instructional Time.* New York: Longman.

Flagg, J. T., Jr. 1965. "The Organizational Climate of Schools: Its Relationship to Pupil Achievement, Size of School, and Teacher Turnover." (Ph.D. dissertation, Rutgers University, 1964). *Dissertation Abstracts* 26:818-19.

Flinders, D. J. 1989. *Voices From the Classroom: Educational Practice Can Inform Policy.* Eugene, OR: ERIC Clearinghouse in Educational Management.

Fonstad, C. 1973. *What Research Says About Schools and School Districts: Factors Related to Effectiveness.* Madison: Wisconsin Department of Public Instruction. (ERIC Document Reproduction Service No. ED 085 892)

Forehand, G. A. and B. Gilmer. 1964. "Environmental Variation in Studies of Organizational Behavior." *Psychological Bulletin* 62:361-82.

Fox, W. F. 1980. *Relationships Between Size of Schools and School Districts and the Cost of Education.* Technical Bulletin No. 1621, U.S. Department of Agriculture, Economics, Statistics and Cooperative Service. (ERIC Document Reproduction Service No. ED 187 029)

Fraser, B. J. 1986. *Classroom Environment.* London: Croom Helm.

Fraser, B. J. and A. J. Rentoul. 1982. "Relationship Between School-Level and Classroom-Level Environment." *Alberta Journal of Educational Research* 28:212-25.

Fraser, B. J., W. W. Welch, and H. J. Walberg. 1986. "Using Secondary Analysis of National Assessment Data to Identify Predictors of Junior High School Students' Outcomes." *Alberta Journal of Educational Research* 32:37-50.

Fraser, B. J., J. C. Williamson, and K. G. Tobin. 1987. "Use of Classroom and School Climate Scales in Evaluating Alternative High Schools." *Teaching and Teacher Education* 3:219-31.

Fullan, M. G. 1990. "Change Processes in Secondary Schools: Toward a More Fundamental Agenda." Pp. 224-55 in *The Contexts of Teacher in Secondary Schools: Teachers' Realities*, edited by M. W. McLaughlin, J. E. Talbert, and N. Bascia. New York: Teachers College Press.

Gamoran, A. 1986. "Instructional and Institutional Effects of Ability Grouping." *Sociology of Education* 59:185-98.

———. 1987. "The Stratification of High School Learning Opportunities." *Sociology of Education* 60:135-55.

Gamoran, A. and M. Berends. 1987. "The Effects of Stratification in Secondary Schools: Synthesis of Survey and Ethnographic Research." *Review of Educational Research* 57:415-35.

Garet, M. and B. DeLany. 1988. "Students, Courses, and Stratification." *Sociology of Education* 1988:61-77.

Garfinkel, H. 1967. *Studies in Ethnomethodology.* Englewood Cliffs, NJ: Prentice-Hall.

Garner, C. L. and S. W. Raudenbush. 1991. "Neighborhood Effects on Educational Attainment: A Multilevel Analysis." *Sociology of Education* 64:251-62.

Gettinger, M. 1989. "Effects of Maximizing Time Spent and Minimizing Time Needed for Learning on Pupil Achievement." *American Educational Research Journal* 26:73-91.

Giroux, H. 1983. *Theory and Resistance in Education: A Pedagogy for the Opposition.* Granby, MA: Bergin & Garvey.

———. 1988a. *Schooling and the Struggle for Public Life: Critical Pedagogy in the Modern Age.* Minneapolis: University of Minnesota Press.

———. 1988b. *Teachers as Intellectuals: Toward a Critical Pedagogy of Learning.* Granby, MA: Bergin & Garvey.

Glasman, N. S. and I. Biniaminov. 1981. "Input-Output Analyses in Schools." *Review of Educational Research* 51:509-39.

Glass, G. V., L. S. Cahen, M. Lee Smith, and N. N. Filby. 1982. *School Class Size: Research and Policy.* Beverly Hills, CA: Sage.

Gonder, P. O. 1981. "Exchanging School and Community Resources." In *Communities and Their Schools*, edited by D. Davies. New York: McGraw-Hill.

Good, T. L. 1979. "Teacher Effectiveness in the Elementary School: What We Know About It Now." *Journal of Teacher Education* 30:52-64.

Good, T. L. and J. E. Brophy. 1986. "School Effects." Pp. 570-602 in *Handbook of Research on Teaching*, edited by M. C. Wittrock. New York: Macmillan.

Goodlad, J. I. 1984. *A Place Called School: Prospects for the Future.* New York: McGraw-Hill.

———. 1987. *The Ecology of School Renewal: Eighty-Sixth Yearbook of the National Society for the Study of Education.* Part I. Chicago: NSSE.

Grant, G. 1982. *Education, Character, and American Schools: Are Effective Schools Good Enough?* Syracuse, NY: Syracuse University.

Greeley, A. M. 1982. *Catholic High Schools and Minority Students.* New Brunswick: Transaction.

Gregory, T. B. and G. R. Smith. 1987. *High Schools as Communities: The Small School Reconsidered.* Bloomington, IN: Phi Delta Kappa Educational Foundation.

Guthrie, J. W., G. B. Kleindorfer, H. M. Levin, and R. T. Stout. 1971. *Schools and Inequality.* Cambridge, MA: MIT Press.

Guttentag, M. and P. Secord. 1983. *Too Many Women: The Sex Ratio Question.* Beverly Hills, CA: Sage.

Habermas, J. 1975. *Legitimation Crisis.* Boston: Beacon.

———. 1987. *Theory of Communicative Action*, translated by T. McCarthy. Boston: Beacon.

Haertel, G. D., H. J. Walberg, and E. H. Haertel. 1981. "Socio-Psychological Environments and Learning: A Quantitative Synthesis." *British Educational Research Journal* 7:27-36.

Haller, E. J. 1985. "Pupil Race and Elementary School Ability Grouping: Are Teachers Biased Against Black Children?" *American Educational Research Journal* 22:465-83.

Hallinan, M. 1984. "Summary and Implications." In *The Social Context of Instruction: Group Organization and Group Processes*, edited by P. L. Peterson, L. C. Wilkinson, and M. Hallinan. Orlando, FL: Academic Press.

———. 1987. "Ability Grouping and Student Learning." Pp. 41-69 in *The Social Organization of Schools: New Conceptualizations of the Learning Process*, edited by M. T. Hallinan. New York: Plenum.

———. 1990. "The Effects of Ability Grouping in Secondary Schools: A Response to Slavin's Best-Evidence Synthesis." *Review of Educational Research* 3:501-4.

Hallinan, M. and A. B. Sorensen. 1983. "The Formation and Stability of Instructional Groups." *American Sociological Review* 48:838-51.

Halpin, A. W. 1966. *Theory and Research in Administration.* New York: Macmillan.

Halpin, A. W. and D. B. Croft. 1963. *The Organizational Climates of Schools.* Chicago: University of Chicago, Midwest Administration Center.

Hamilton, S. F. 1983. "Synthesis of Research on the Social Side of Schooling." *Educational Leadership* 40:5:65-72.

Hanks, M. P. and B. K. Eckland. 1976. "Athletics and Social Participation in the Educational Attainment Process." *Sociology of Education* 49:271-94.

Hanushek, E. A. 1971. "Teacher Characteristics and Gains in Student Achievement: Estimation Using Micro-Data." *American Economic Review* 61:280-88.

———. 1972. *Education and Race: An Analysis of the Educational Production Process.* Lexington, MA: Lexington.

———. 1986. "The Economics of Schooling: Production and Efficiency in Public Schools." *Journal of Economic Literature* 24:1141-77.

———. 1989. "The Impact of Differential Expenditures on School Performance." *Educational Researcher* 18(May):45-51, 62.

Harnischfeger, A. and D. E. Wiley. 1980. "Determinants of Pupil Opportunity." In *The Analysis of Educational Productivity. Vol. 1, Issues in Microanalysis*, edited by R. Dreeben and J. A. Thomas. Cambridge, MA: Ballinger.

Hauser, R. M. 1971. *Socioeconomic Background and Educational Performance.* Washington, DC: American Sociological Association.

Heck, S. F. and C. R. Williams. 1984. *The Complex Roles of the Teachers.* New York: Teachers College Press.

Hedrick, D. W. 1984. "Student Achievement and Instructional Time: A Simultaneous Equations Approach." Ph.D. dissertation, University of Oregon.

Hellriegel, D. and J. W. Slocum. 1974. "Organizational Climate: Measures, Research and Contingencies." *Academy of Management Journal* 17:255-80.

Henderson, A. T. 1988. "Good News: An Ecologically Balanced Approach to Academic Improvement." *Educational Horizons* 66:60-62.

Herndon, J. 1968. *The Way It Spozed to Be.* New York: Simon & Schuster.

———. 1971. *How to Survive in Your Native Land.* New York: Bantam.

Heyns, B. 1974. "Social Selection and Stratification Within Schools." *American Journal of Sociology* 79:1434-51.

———. 1978. *Summer Learning.* New York: Academic Press.

Hoffer, T., A. M. Greeley, and J. S. Coleman. 1987. "Catholic High School Effects on Achievement Growth." In *Comparing Public and Private Schools. Vol. 2, School Achievement*, edited by E. H. Haertel, T. James, and H. M. Levin. New York: Falmer.

Holland, A. and T. Andre. 1987. "Participation in Extracurricular Activities in Secondary School: What Is Known, What Needs to Be Known." *Review of Educational Research* 57:437-66.

Holt, J. 1964. *How Children Fail.* New York: Pitman.

———. 1967. *How Children Learn.* New York: Pitman.

Homans, G. 1961. *Social Behavior: Its Elementary Forms.* New York: Harcourt Brace.

Hoy, W. K., C. J. Tarter, and R. B. Kottkamp. 1991. *Open Schools / Healthy Schools: Measuring Organizational Climate.* Newbury Park, CA: Sage.

Huber, J. D. 1983. "Comparison of Disciplinary Concerns in Small and Large Schools." *The Small School Forum* 4:7-9.

Huling, L. 1980. "How School Size Affects Student Participation, Alienation." *NASSP Bulletin* 64:13-18.

Husen, T. and A. Tuijnman. 1991. "The Contribution of Formal Schooling to the Increase in Intellectual Capital." *Educational Researcher* 20(October):17-25.

Irvine, D. J. 1979. "Factors Associated With School Effectiveness." *Educational Technology* 19: 53-5.

Jackson, P. 1968. *Life in Classrooms.* New York: Holt, Rinehart & Winston.

Jencks, C. et al. 1972. *Inequality: A Reassessment of the Effect of Family and Schooling in America.* New York: Basic Books.

———. 1979. *Who Gets Ahead? The Determinants of Economic Success in America.* New York: Basic Books.

Jess, J. D. 1989. "A Local School Perspective." In *Rural Education: A Changing Landscape*, edited by J. D. Sern. Washington, DC: US Department of Education, Office of Educational Research and Improvement.

Jessup, D. K. 1985. *Teachers, Unions, and Change: A Comparative Study.* New York: Praeger.

Jones, A. P. and L. R. James. 1979. "Psychological Climate: Dimensions and Relationships of Individual and Aggregated Work Environment

Perceptions." *Organizational Behavior and Human Performance* 23:201-50.
Joyce, B., R. Hersh, and M. McKibbin. 1983. *The Structure of School Improvement.* New York: Longman.
Kachel, D. 1989. "How the Amish Educate Their Children: Can We Learn From Them?" *Educational Horizons* 67:92-97.
Kalis, M. C. 1980. "Teaching Experience: Its Effect on School Climate, Teacher Morale." *NASSP Bulletin* 64:89-102.
Kasarda, J. D. 1974. "Community Attachment in Mass Society." *American Sociological Review* 39:328-39.
Katz, M. B. 1968. *The Irony of Early School Reform: Educational Innovation in Mid-nineteenth Century Massachusetts.* Cambridge, MA: Harvard University Press.
Kaufman, H. F. 1959. "Toward an Interactional Conception of Community." *Social Forces* 38:8-17.
Kelly, D. H. 1975. "Tracking and Its Impact on Self-Esteem: A Neglected Dimension." *Education* 96:2-9.
Kierstad, R. 1963. "A Comparison and Evaluation of Two Methods of Organization for the Teaching of Reading." *Journal of Educational Research* 56:317-21.
Kiesling, H. J. 1968. *High School Size and Cost Factors.* Report of Project No. 6-1590. Washington, DC: U.S. Department of Health, Education and Welfare.
Kilgore, S. B. 1991. "The Organizational Context of Tracking in Schools." *American Sociological Review* 56:189-203.
Kleinert, E. J. 1969. "Effects of High School Size on Student Activity Participation." *NASSP Bulletin* 53:34-46.
Klitgaard, R. E. and G. Hall. 1973. *Are There Unusually Effective Schools?* Santa Monica, CA: Rand. (ERIC Document Reproduction Service No. ED 085 402)
Kounin, J. 1970. *Discipline and Group Management in Classrooms.* New York: Holt, Rinehart & Winston.
Koziol, K. 1990. "Uniting a Community for Collaboration: A Conversation With Sister Jean Patrices Harrington." *Educational Horizons* 68:179-81.
Kozol, J. 1967. *Death at an Early Age: The Destruction of the Hearts and Minds of Negro Children in the Boston Public Schools.* Boston: Houghton Mifflin.
Krauss, I. 1964. "Sources of Educational Aspirations Among Working-Class Youth." *American Sociological Review* 29:867-79.
Krietlow, B. 1962, 1966, 1971. *Long Term Study of Educational Effectiveness of Newly Formed Centralized School Districts in Rural Areas.* Reports 1, 2, and 3. Madison: University of Wisconsin.

Kulik, C. L. and J. A. Kulik. 1982. "Effects of Ability Grouping on Secondary School Students: A Meta-Analysis of Evaluation Findings." *American Educational Research Journal* 19:415-28.

———. 1984. "Effects of Accelerated Instruction on Students." *Review of Educational Research* 54:409-25.

Lareau, A. 1989. *Home Advantage.* Philadelphia: Falmer.

Lee, V. E. and A. S. Bryk. 1986. "Effects of Single-Sex Secondary Schools on Student Achievement and Attitudes." *Journal of Educational Psychology* 78:381-95.

———. 1988. "Curriculum Tracking as Mediating the Social Distribution of High School Achievement." *Sociology of Education* 61:78-94.

———. 1989. "A Multilevel Model of the Social Distribution of High School Achievement." *Sociology of Education* 62:172-92.

Leechor, C. 1988. "How High and Low Achieving Students Differentially Benefit From Working Together in Cooperative Small Groups." Ph.D. dissertation, Stanford University.

Leitch, M. L. and S. S. Tangri. 1988. "Barriers to Home-School Collaboration." *Educational Horizons* 66:70-74.

Levin, H. M. 1980. "Educational Production Theory and Teacher Inputs." In *The Analysis of Educational Productivity. Vol. 2, Issues in Macroanalysis*, edited by C. E. Bidwell and D. M. Windham. Cambridge, MA: Ballinger.

———. 1983. "Commentary: Reawakening the Vigor of Urban Schools." *Education Week* 2:34, 24.

Levine, D. U. 1990. "Update on Effective Schools: Findings and Implications From Research and Practice." *Journal of Negro Education* 59:577-84.

Lewin, K. 1935. *A Dynamic Theory of Personality.* New York: McGraw-Hill.

———. 1951. *Field Theory in Social Science.* New York: Harper.

Lightfoot, S. L. 1978. *Worlds Apart: Relationships Between Families and Schools.* New York: Basic Books.

———. 1983. *The Good High School: Portraits of Character and Culture.* New York: Basic Books.

Lipsitz, J. 1984. *Successful Schools for Young Adolescents.* New Brunswick, NJ: Transaction.

Lutz, F. W. 1990. "Reforming Education American Style." Pp. 110-34 in *Shaping the Superintendency: A Reexamination of Callahan and the Cult of Efficiency.* New York: Teachers College Press.

Madaus, G. F., P. W. Airasian, and T. Kellaghan. 1980. *School Effectiveness: A Reassessment of the Evidence.* New York: McGraw-Hill.

Mahard, R. E. and R. L. Crain. 1983. "Research on Minority Achievement in Desegregated Schools." In *The Consequences of School Desegrega-*

*tion*, edited by C. H. Rossell and W. D. Hawley. Philadelphia: Temple University Press.

Marsh, H. W. and J. W. Parker. 1984. "Determinants of Student Self-Concept: Is It Better to Be a Relatively Large Fish in a Small Pond Even If You Don't Learn to Swim as Well?" *Journal of Personality and Social Psychology* 47:213-31.

Marx, K. 1845/1965. "Theses on Feuerbach." In *Basic Problems of Marx's Philosophy*, edited by N. Rotenstreich. Indianapolis: Bobbs-Merrill.

———. 1844/1963. "Economic and Philosophic Manuscripts." Pp. 66-219 in *Karl Marx: Early Writings*, edited by T. B. Bottomore. New York: McGraw Hill.

McBeath, G., J. Kleinfeld, W. G. McDiarmid, E. D. Coon, and C. E. Shepro. 1983. *Patterns of Control in Rural Alaska Education*. Fairbanks: University of Alaska, Center for Cross-Cultural Studies.

McCloskey, M. and T. Harrison. 1983. "Community Education: A Process for Involvement." *Educational Horizons* 61:133-36.

McDill, E. L., E. D. Meyers, Jr., and L. C. Rigsby. 1967. "Institutional Effects on the Academic Behavior of High School Students." *Sociology of Education* 40:181-99.

McDill, E. L. and L. C. Rigsby. 1973. *Structure and Process in Secondary Schools*. Baltimore, MD: John Hopkins University Press.

McDill, E. L., L. C. Rigsby, and E. D. Meyers, Jr. 1969. "Educational Climates of High Schools: Their Effects and Sources." *American Journal of Sociology* 74:567-86.

McLaren, P. 1989. *Life in Schools: An Introduction to Critical Pedagogy in the Foundations of Education*. New York: Longman.

McLaughlin, M. W. and J. E. Talbert. 1990. "The Contexts in Question: The Secondary School Workplace." Pp. 1-4 in *The Contexts of Teacher in Secondary Schools: Teachers' Realities*, edited by M. W. McLaughlin, J. E. Talbert, and N. Bascia. New York: Teachers College Press.

McPartland, J. M. and E. L. McDill. 1982. "Control and Differentiation in the Structure of American Education." *Sociology of Education* 55:77-88.

McPherson, G. H. 1972. *Small Town Teacher.* Cambridge, MA: Harvard University Press.

Metz, M. H. 1978. *Classrooms and Corridors: The Crisis of Authority in Desegregated Secondary Schools.* Berkeley: University of California Press.

———. 1986. *Different by Design: The Context and Character of Three Magnet Schools.* London: Routledge & Kegan Paul.

———. 1990. "How Social Class Differences Shape Teachers' Work." Pp. 40-107 in *The Contexts of Teacher in Secondary Schools: Teachers'*

*Realities*, edited by M. W. McLaughlin, J. E. Talbert, and N. Bascia. New York: Teachers College Press.

Meyer, J. W. 1970. "High School Effects on College Intentions." *American Journal of Sociology* 76:59-70.

———. 1980. "Levels of the Educational System and Schooling Effects." In *The Analysis of Educational Productivity. Vol. 2, Issues in Microanalysis,* edited by C. E. Bidwell and D. M. Windham. Cambridge, MA: Ballinger.

Meyer, J. W. and B. Rowan. 1977. "Institutionalized Organizations: Formal Structure as Myth and Ceremony." *American Journal of Sociology* 83:340-63.

———. 1978. "The Structure of Educational Organizations." Pp. 78-109 in *Environments and Organizations,* edited by M. W. Meyer and associates. San Francisco: Jossey-Bass.

Michael, J. A. 1961. "High School Climates and Plans for Entering College." *Public Opinion Quarterly* 25:585-95.

Michelson, S. 1970. "The Association of Teacher Resources With Children's Characteristics." In *Do Teachers Make a Difference?* Washington, DC: U.S. Department of Health, Education and Welfare, Office of Education.

Minzey, J. D. 1981. "Community Education in the United States." Pp. 269-95 in *Communities and Their Schools*, edited by D. Davies. New York: McGraw-Hill.

Miranda, W. 1983. "Using Community Resources in the Classroom." *Educational Horizons* 61:137-40.

Miskel, C. and R. Ogawa. 1988. "Work Motivation, Job Satisfaction, and Climate." In *Handbook of Research on Educational Administration*, edited by N. J. Boyan. New York: Longman.

Mitchell, J. V., Jr. 1967. *A Study of High School Learning Environments and Their Impact on Students.* Report from U.S. Office of Education Project No. 5-8032. Rochester, NY: University of Rochester.

Moles, O. C. 1982. "Synthesis of Recent Research on Parent Participation in Children's Education." *Educational Leadership* 40:44-47.

Moorhouse, W. F. 1964. "Interclass Grouping for Reading Instruction." *Elementary School Journal* 64:280-86.

Moos, R. H. 1976. *The Human Context: Environmental Determinants of Behavior.* New York: John Wiley.

———. 1979. *Evaluating Educational Environments.* San Francisco: Jossey-Bass.

———. 1987. "Person-Environment Congruence in Work, School, and Health Care Settings." *Journal of Vocational Behavior* 31:231-47.

Moos, R. H. and P. M. Insel. 1974. *Issues in Social Ecology: Human Milieus.* Palo Alto, CA: National Press Books.

Morgan, D. L. and D. F. Alwin. 1980. "When Less Is More: School Size and Student Social Participation." *Social Psychology Quarterly* 43:241-52.

Morris, V. P. 1969. "An Evaluation of Pupil Achievement in a Nongraded Primary Plan After Three, and Also Five Years of Instruction." *Dissertation Abstracts* 29:3809A. (University Microfilms No. 69-7352)

Mortimore, P., P. Sammons, L. Stoll, D. Lewis, and R. Ecob. 1988. *School Matters.* Berkeley: University of California Press.

Murnane, R. J. 1975. *Impact of School Resources on the Learning of Inner City Children.* Cambridge, MA: Ballinger.

Murray, H. 1938. *Explorations in Personality.* New York: Oxford University Press.

Natriello, G., A. Pallas, and K. Alexander. 1989. "On the Right Track? Curriculum and Academic Achievement." *Sociology of Education* 62:109-18.

Nelson, J. I. 1972. "High School Context and College Plans: The Impact of Social Structure on Aspirations." *American Sociological Review* 37:143-48.

Newmann, F. M. 1981. "Reducing Student Alienation in High Schools: Implications of Theory." *Harvard Educational Review* 51:546-64.

Newmann, F. M., R. A. Rutter, and M. S. Smith. 1989. "Organizational Factors That Affect School Sense of Efficacy, Community, and Expectations." *Sociology of Education* 62:221-38.

Oakes, J. 1985. *Keeping Track: How Schools Structure Inequality.* New Haven, CT: Yale University Press.

———. 1987. "Tracking in Secondary Schools: A Contextual Perspective." *Educational Psychology* 22:129-53.

Olsen, E. G., ed. 1953. *The Modern Community School.* New York: Appleton-Century-Crofts.

O'Reilly, R. 1975. "Classroom Climate and Achievement in Secondary School Mathematics Classes." *Alberta Journal of Educational Research* 21:241-48.

Owens, R. G. and C. R. Steinhoff. 1989. "Group Leadership Skills of School Principals: The Present Knowledge Base and Beyond." Paper presented at the annual meeting of the UCEA, Scottsdale, AZ.

Pace, C. R. and G. G. Stern. 1958. "An Approach to the Measurement of Psychological Characteristics of College Environments." *Journal of Educational Psychology* 49:269-77.

Parks, G. A., P. J. Ross, and A. E. Just. 1982. "Education." In *Rural Society in the U.S.: Issues for the 1980's*, edited by D. A. Dillman and D. J. Hobbs. Boulder, CO: Westview.

Parsons, T. 1958. "Some Ingredients of a General Theory of Social Organization." In *Administrative Theory in Education*, edited by A. W. Halpin. Chicago: Midwest Administration Center.

———. 1959. "The School Class as a Social System." *Harvard Educational Review* 29:297-318.

———. 1960. *Structure and Process in Modern Societies*. Glencoe, IL: Free Press.

Parsons, T., R. F. Bales, and E. Shils. 1954. *Working Papers in the Theory of Action*. Glencoe, IL: Free Press.

Parsons, T. and E. Shils. 1952. *Towards a General Theory of Action*. Cambridge, MA: Harvard University Press.

Patchen, M. 1982. *Black-White Contact in Schools: Its Social and Academic Effects*. West Lafayette, IN: Purdue University Press.

Pedersen, E., T. A. Faucher, and W. W. Eaton. 1978. "A New Perspective on the Effects of First-Grade Teachers on Children's Subsequent Adult Status." *Harvard Educational Review* 48:1-31.

Peng, S. S., J. P. Bailey, Jr., and B. K. Ekland. 1977. "Access to Education: Results From the National Longitudinal Study of the High School Class of 1972." *Educational Researcher* 88:3-7.

Peng, S. S. et al. 1982. *Effective High Schools: What Are Their Attributes?* Washington, DC: National Center for Education Statistics, Office of Educational Research and Improvement.

Pepple, J. D., D. A. Law, and S. C. Kallembach. 1990. "A Vision of Rural Education for 2001." *Educational Horizons* 69:50-58.

Perrone, V. et al. 1985. *Portraits of High Schools: A Supplement to High School: A Report on Secondary Education in America*. New York: Carnegie Foundation.

Peshkin, A. 1978. *Growing up American: Schooling and the Survival of Community*. Chicago: University of Chicago Press.

———. 1982. *The Imperfect Union: School Consolidation and Community Conflict*. Chicago: University of Chicago Press.

Pettigrew, T. F. and R. L. Green. 1976. "School Desegregation in Large Cities: A Critique of the Coleman 'White Flight' Thesis." *Harvard Educational Review* 46:1-53.

Phi Delta Kappa. 1980. *Why Do Some Urban Schools Succeed? The Phi Delta Kappa Study of Exceptional Urban Elementary Schools*. Bloomington, IN: Author.

Power, T. J. and K. L. Bartholomew. 1987. "Family-School Relationship Patterns: An Ecological Assessment." *School Psychology Review* 16:498-512.

Provus, M. M. 1960. "Ability Grouping in Arithmetic." *Elementary School Journal* 64:387-92.

Puff, F. 1978. *Instructional Variables and Student Achievement in Reading and Mathematics: A Synthesis of Recent Process-Produce*

*Research*. Philadelphia: Research for Better Schools, Inc. (ERIC Document Reproduction Service No. ED 189 135)

Purkey, S. and M. Smith. 1982. *Effective Schools: A Review*. Madison: University of Wisconsin, Center for Educational Research.

Raffel, J. A. 1980. *The Politics of School Desegregation: The Metropolitan Remedy in Delaware*. Philadelphia: Temple University Press.

Raymond, R. 1968. "Determinants of Primary and Secondary Education in West Virginia." *Journal of Human Resources* 3:450-70.

Rees, P. H. 1970. "Concepts of Social Space: Toward an Urban Social Geography." Pp. 306-94 in *Geographic Perspectives on Urban Systems*, edited by B. Berry and F. Horton. Englewood Cliffs, NJ: Prentice-Hall.

Riordan, C. 1990. *Girls and Boys in School: Together or Separate?* New York: Teachers College Press.

Rogoff, N. 1961. "Local Social Structure and Educational Selection." In *Education, Economy, and Society*, edited by A. H. Holsey, J. Floud, and C. Arnold Anderson. New York: Free Press.

Rosenbaum, J. E. 1976. *Making Inequality*. New York: John Wiley.

———. 1980. "Track Misperceptions and Frustrated College Plans: An Analysis of the Effects of Tracks and Track Perceptions in the National Longitudinal Survey." *Sociology of Education* 53:74-88.

Rosenfeld, S. A. and J. P. Sher. 1977. "The Urbanization of Rural Schools, 1840-1970." In *Education in Rural America: A Reassessment of Conventional Wisdom*, edited by J. P. Sher. Boulder, CO: Westview.

Rosenholtz, S. J. 1985. "Effective Schools: Interpreting the Evidence." *American Journal of Education* 94:352-87.

———. 1989. *Teachers' Workplace: The Social Organization of Schools*. New York: Longman.

Rosenholtz, S. J. and C. Simpson. 1990. "Workplace Conditions and the Rise and Fall of Teachers' Commitment." *Sociology of Education* 63: 241-57.

Rosenshine, B. V. 1971. *Teaching Behaviors and Student Achievement*. London: National Foundation for Educational Research.

———. 1979. "Content, Time, and Direct Instruction." Pp. 11-56 in *Research on Teaching: Concepts, Findings, and Implications*, edited by P. L. Peterson and H. J. Walberg. Berkeley, CA: McCutchan.

———. 1983. "Teaching Functions in Instructional Programs." *Elementary School Journal* 83:335-51.

Rosenshine, B. V. and D. Berliner. 1976. "Academic Engaged Time." *British Journal of Teacher Education* 4:3-16.

Rossell, C. H. 1990. *The Carrot or the Stick for School Desegregation Policy: Magnet Schools or Forced Busing*. Philadelphia: Temple University Press.

Rossmiller, R. A. 1982. "Use of Resources: Does It Influence Student Achievement?" *Educational Perspectives* 21:23-32.

Rowan, B. 1990. "Commitment and Control: Alternative Strategies for the Organizational Design of Schools." *Review of Research in Education* 16:353-89.

Rowan, B., S. Bosset, and D. Dwyer. 1983. "Research on Effective Schools: A Cautionary Note." *Educational Researcher* 12:24-31.

Rowan, B. and A. Miracle. 1983. "Systems of Ability Grouping and the Stratification of Achievement in Elementary Schools." *Sociology of Education* 56:133-44.

Rutter, M., B. Maughan, P. Mortimore, J. Ouston, and A. Smith. 1979. *Fifteen Thousand Hours: Secondary Schools and Their Effects on Children.* Cambridge, MA: Harvard University Press.

St. John, N. 1975. *School Desegregation: Outcomes for Children.* New York: John Wiley.

Sargeant, J. C. 1967. *Organizational Climate of High School.* Minneapolis: University of Minnesota, Educational Research and Development Council.

Schaefer, W. and C. Olexa. 1971. *Tracking and Opportunity.* Scranton, PA: Chandler.

Schein, E. H. 1990. "Organizational Culture." *American Psychologist* 45:109-19.

Schieber, J. A., B. J. Drummel, J. Gundy, K. W. Iverson, D. A. Johnson, M. J. Manning, and P. Riordan. 1979. "The Effect of Class Size on Student Achievement." *Illinois School Research and Development* 15:121-26.

Schmuck, P. and R. Schmuck. 1990. "Democratic Participation in Small-Town Schools." *Educational Researcher* 19(November):14-19.

Schneider, B. 1975. "Organizational Climate: An Essay." *Personnel Psychology* 28:447-79.

Schneider, B. and A. E. Reichers. 1983. "On the Etiology of Climates." *Personnel Psychology* 36:19-40.

Schneider, J. M., J. D. Glasheen, and D. W. Hadley. 1979. "Secondary School Participation, Institutional Socialization, and Student Achievement." *Urban Education* 14:285-302.

Schofield, J. W. 1982. *Black and White in School: Trust, Tension, or Tolerance?* New York: Praeger.

———. 1991. "School Desegregation and Intergroup Relations: A Review of the Literature." *Review of Research in Education* 17:335-409.

Schofield, J. W. and H. A. Sagar. 1983. "Desegregation, School Practices, and Student Race Relations." In *The Consequences of School Desegregation*, edited by C. H. Rossell and W. D. Hawley. Philadelphia: Temple University Press.

Sciulli, D. and D. Gerstein. 1985. "Social Theory and Talcott Parsons in the 1980s." *Annual Review of Sociology* 11:369-87.

Seeley, D. and R. Schwartz. 1981. "Debureaucratizing Public Education: The Experience of New York and Boston." In *Communities and Their Schools*, edited by D. Davies. New York: McGraw-Hill.

Segal, D. and O. J. Schwarm. 1957. *Retention in High Schools in Large Cities.* A Report to the U. S. Department of Health, Education and Welfare. Washington, DC: Government Printing Office.

Sewell, W. H. and J. M. Armer. 1966. "Neighborhood Context and College Plans." *American Sociological Review* 31:159-68.

Sewell, W. H. and V. P. Shah. 1968. "Social Class, Parental Encouragement, and Educational Aspirations." *American Journal of Sociology* 73:559-72.

Shapiro, S. 1989. *Between Capitalism and Democracy: Educational Policy and the Crisis of the Welfare State.* New York: Bergin & Garvey.

Shavit, Y. and D. L. Featherman. 1988. "Schooling, Tracking, and Teenage Intelligence." *Sociology of Education* 61:42-51.

Shea, B. M. 1976. "Schooling and Its Antecedents: Substantive and Methodological Issues in the Status Attainment Process." *Review of Educational Research* 46:463-526.

Sher, J. P. and R. B. Tompkins. 1977. "Economy, Efficiency, and Equality: The Myths of Rural School and District Consolidation." Pp. 43-80 in *Education in Rural America: A Reassessment of Conventional Wisdom*, edited by J. P. Sher. Boulder, CO: Westview.

Shipman, M. D. 1968. *The Sociology of the School.* London: Longman.

Silberman, C. E. 1970. *Crisis in the Classroom.* New York: Random House.

Silver, M. B. 1990. "The Conpact Project: Bringing Business and School Together." *Educational Horizons* 68:172-78.

Simmel, G. 1923/1955. *Conflict and the Web of Group Affiliations.* Glencoe, IL: Free Press.

———. 1908/1950. *The Sociology of Georg Simmel.* Glencoe, IL: Free Press.

Sinclair, R. L. 1970. "Elementary School Educational Environments: Toward Schools That Are Responsive to Students." *National Elementary Principal* 49:53-58.

Sizer, T. R. 1984. *Horace's Compromise: The Dilemma of the American High School.* Boston: Houghton Mifflin.

Skapski, M. K. 1960. "Ungraded Primary Reading Program: An Objective Evaluation." *Elementary School Journal* 61:41-45.

Slavin, R. E. 1987a. "Ability Grouping and Student Achievement in Elementary Schools: A Best-Evidence Synthesis." *Review of Educational Research* 57:293-336.

———. 1987b. "A Theory of School and Classroom Organization." *Educational Psychologist* 22:89-108.

———. 1990a. "Ability Grouping in Secondary Schools: A Response to Hallinan." *Review of Educational Research* 60:505-7.

———. 1990b. "Achievement Effects of Ability Grouping in Secondary Schools: A Best-Evidence Synthesis." *Review of Educational Research* 60:471-99.

———. 1990c. *Cooperative Learning: Theory, Research, and Practice.* Englewood Cliffs, NJ: Prentice-Hall.

Slavin, R. E. and N. L. Karweit. 1985. "Effects of Whole Class, Ability Grouped, and Individualized Instruction on Mathematics Achievement." *American Educational Research Journal* 22:351-67.

Smith, M. S. 1972. "Equality of Educational Opportunity: The Basic Findings Reconsidered." Pp. 230-342 in *On Equality of Educational Opportunity*, edited by F. Mosteller and D. P. Moynihan. New York: Vintage.

Smith, W. M. 1960. "The Effect of Intra-Class Ability Grouping on Arithmetic Achievement in Grades Two Through Five." *Dissertation Abstracts International* 21:563-64.

Sorensen, A. B. 1970. "Organizational Differentiation of Students and Educational Opportunity." *Sociology of Education* 43:355-76.

———. 1987. "The Organizational Differentiation of Students in Schools as an Opportunity Structure." In *The Social Organization of Schools: New Conceptualizations of the Learning Process*, edited by M. T. Hallinan. New York: Plenum.

Sorensen, A. B. and M. T. Hallinan. 1986. "Effects of Ability Grouping on Growth in Academic Achievement." *American Educational Research Journal* 23:519-42.

Spencer, B. D. and D. E. Wiley. 1981. "The Sense and the Nonsense of School Effectiveness." *Journal of Policy Analysis and Management* 1:43-52.

Spring, J. M. 1976. *The Sorting Machine: National Educational Policy Since 1945.* New York: David McKay.

Stallings, J., J. Fairweather, and M. Needels. 1978. *A Study of Basic Reading Skills Taught in Secondary Schools.* Palo Alto, CA: SRI International.

Steinitz, V. A. and E. R. Solomon. 1986. *Starting Out: Class and Community in the Lives of Working-Class Youth.* Philadelphia: Temple University Press.

Stevenson, D. L. 1991. "Deviant Students as a Collective Resource in Classroom Control." *Sociology of Education* 64:127-33.

Stevenson, D. L. and D. P. Baker. 1987. "The Family-School Relation and the Child's School Performance." *Child Development* 58:1348-57.

Stockard, J. and M. M. Johnson. 1992. *Sex and Gender in Society.* Englewood Cliffs, NJ: Prentice-Hall.

Stringfield, S., C. Teddlie, and S. Suarez. 1985. "Classroom Interaction in Effective and Ineffective Schools: Preliminary Results From Phase III of the Louisiana School Effectiveness Study." *Journal of Classroom Interaction* 20:31-37.

Summers, A. A. and B. L. Wolfe. 1977. "Do Schools Make a Difference?" *American Economic Review* 65:639-52.

Tagiuri, R. 1968. "The Concept of Organizational Climate." In *Organizational Climate: Explorations of a Concept,* edited by R. Tagiuri and G. H. Litwin. Boston: Harvard University Press.

Tagiuri, R. and G. H. Litwin, eds. 1968. *Organizational Climate: Explorations of a Concept.* Boston: Harvard University Press.

Teddlie, C., P. C. Kirby, and S. Stringfield. 1989. "Effective Versus Ineffective Schools: Observable Differences in the Classroom." *American Journal of Education,* May, pp. 221-36.

Tornatzky, L. G., W. B. Brookover, D. V. Hathaway, S. K. Miller, and J. Passalacqua. 1980. "Changing School Climate: A Case Study in Implementation." *Urban Review* 15:49-64.

Trickett, E. J. 1978. "Toward a Social-Ecological Conception of Adolescent Socialization: Normative Data on Contrasting Types of Public School Classrooms." *Child Development* 49:408-14.

Tucker, H. J. and L. H. Zeigler. 1980. *Professional Versus the Public: Attitudes, Communication, and Response in Local School Districts.* New York: Longman.

Turner, C. C. and J. M. Thrasher. 1970. *School Size Does Make a Difference.* San Diego, CA: Institute for Educational Management.

Turner, R. 1964. *The Social Context of Ambition.* San Francisco: Chandler.

Turner, R., G. Camill, R. Kroc, and J. Hoover. 1986. "Policy Strategies, Teacher Salary Incentive, and Student Achievement: An Explanatory Model." *Educational Researcher* 15:5-11.

Tyack, D. 1974. *The One Best System.* Cambridge, MA: Harvard University Press.

Tyler, W. B. 1985. "The Organizational Structure of the School." *Annual Review of Sociology* 11:49-73.

Urich, T. and R. Batchelder. 1979. "Turning an Urban High School Around." *Phi Delta Kappan* 61:206-9.

Vanfossen, B. E., J. D. Jones, and J. Z. Spade. 1987. "Curriculum Tracking and Status Maintenance." *Sociology of Education* 60:104-22.

Walberg, H. 1969a. "Predicting Class Learning: An Approach to the Class as a Social System." *American Educational Research Journal* 6:529-42.

———. 1969b. "Social Environment as a Mediator of Classroom Learning." *Journal of Educational Psychology* 60:443-48.

———. 1975. "Structural and Affective Aspects of Classroom Climate." *Psychology in the Schools* 5:247-53.

———., ed. 1979. *Educational Environments and Effects: Evaluation, Policy, and Productivity.* Berkeley, CA: McCutchan.

Walberg, H. and G. Anderson. 1968. "Classroom Climate and Individual Learning." *Journal of Educational Psychology* 59:414-19.

———. 1972. "Properties of Achievement in Urban Classes." *Journal of Educational Psychology* 61:381-85.

Walberg, H. J. and W. J. Fowler, Jr. 1987. "Expenditure and Size Efficiencies of Public School Districts." *Educational Researcher* 16(October):5-13.

Waller, W. 1932. *The Sociology of Teaching.* New York: John Wiley.

Weber, G. 1971. *Inner City Children Can Be Taught to Read: Four Successful Schools.* Occasional Paper 18. Washington, DC: Council for Basic Education.

Weber, M. 1946. *From Max Weber.* New York: Oxford University Press.

———. 1968. *Economy and Society.* Berkeley: University of California Press.

Weick, K. E. 1976. "Educational Organizations as Loosely Coupled Systems." *Administrative Science Quarterly* 21:1-19.

Weinberg, M. 1983. *The Search for Quality Integrated Education: Policy and Research on Minority Students in School and College.* Westport, CT: Greenwood.

Weinstein, C. S. 1979. "The Physical Environment of the School: A Review of the Research." *Review of Educational Research* 49:577-610.

Wellman, B. 1979. "The Community Question: The Intimate Networks of East Yorkers." *American Journal of Sociology* 84:1201-31.

Wentzel, K. R. 1991. "Social Competence at School: Relation Between Social Responsibility and Academic Achievement." *Review of Educational Research* 61:1-24.

Wicker, A. W. 1968. "Undermanning, Performances, and Students' Subjective Experiences in Behavior Settings of Large and Small High Schools." *Journal of Personality and Social Psychology* 10:255-61.

———. 1969. "Cognitive Complexity, School Size, and Participation in School Behavior Settings: A Test of the Frequency of Interaction Hypothesis." *Journal of Educational Psychology* 60:200-203.

———. 1973. "Undermanning Theory and Research: Implications for the Study of Psychological and Behavioral Effects of Excess Human Populations." *Representative Research in Social Psychology* 4:185-206.

Wilkinson, L. C. 1988. "Grouping Children for Learning: Implications for Kindergarten Education." *Review of Research in Education* 15:203-23.

Willems, E. 1967. "Sense of Obligation to High School Activities as Related to School Size and Marginality of Students." *Child Development* 38:1247-60.

Williams, M. R. 1989. *Neighborhood Organizing for Urban School Reform.* New York: Teachers College Press.

Williams, P. 1980. "Laws Prohibiting Sex Discrimination in the Schools." Pp. 143-64 in *Sex Equity in Education*, edited by J. Stockard, P. A. Schmuck, K. Kempner, P. Williams, S. K. Edson, and M. A. Smith. New York: Academic Press.

Willis, P. 1977. *Learning to Labor.* London: Saxon House.

Willower, D. J. 1977. "Schools and Pupil Control." In *Educational Organization and Administration,* edited by D. Erickson. Berkeley, CA: McCutchan.

Willower, D. J., T. J. Eidell, and W. K. Hoy. 1967. *The School and Pupil Control Ideology.* University Park: Pennsylvania State University.

Wilson, A. B. 1959. "Residential Segregation of Social Classes and Aspirations of High School Boys." *American Sociological Review* 24:836-45.

Wimpelberg, R. K. 1986. "Bureaucratic and Cultural Images in the Management of More and Less Effective Schools." Paper presented at the annual meeting of the American Educational Research Association, San Francisco, CA, April.

Wirt, F. M. and M. W. Kirst. 1982. *The Politics of Education: Schools in Conflict.* Berkeley, CA: McCutchan.

Wynne, E. A. 1980. *Looking at Schools: Good, Bad and Indifferent.* Lexington, MA: Lexington.

Young, B. S. 1980. "Principals Can Be Promoters of Teaching Effectiveness." *Thrust for Educational Leadership* 9:11-12.

Young, R. 1990. *A Critical Theory of Education: Habermas and Our Children's Future.* New York: Teachers College Press.

Zeigler, H. and M. K. Jennings, with the assistance of G. W. Peak. 1974. *Governing American Schools.* North Scituate, MA: Duxbury.

Zeigler, H. and H. J. Tucker. 1981. "Who Governs American Education: One More Time." Pp. 33-57 in *Communities and Their Schools*, edited by D. Davies. New York: McGraw-Hill.

# Author Index

# Subject Index